THE MOST

VALUABLE

BOOK

EVER PUBLISHED

IMPORTANT NOTICE

NOTICE:This manual is intended as a reference volume only, not as a medical guide or a reference for self-treatment. You should always seek competent medical advice from a doctor if you suspect a problem.
This book is intended as an educational device to keep you informed of the latest medical knowledge. It is not intended to serve as a substitute for changing the treatment advice of your doctor. You should never make medical changes without first consulting your doctor.

Printed in the United States of America

0 9 8 7 6 5 4 3 2 1

TABLE OF CONTENTS

Personal, financial and Lifestyle Section

Introduction

Who would have enough guts to write a book called, *The Most Valuable Book Ever Written*? A book with a title that powerful promises an awful lot to its readers. *The Most Valuable Book Ever Written* would have to deliver page after page of information so extraordinary that it would literally change the lives of everyone who reads it.

Well, guess what? This book not only lives up to its title, it delivers on each and every page!

That's right. On any give page within this book may the very answer you have been looking for your entire life. Whether it's a health care issue, a financial problem or a change of lifestyle, *The Most Valuable Book Ever Written* may provide you with the very key you have been seeking for years, perhaps your entire life.

In producing this book, we did not shy away from some of the toughest problems in life. Take incurable medical conditions, for example. We decided not to take a tone of surrender or defeat in our attempts to find solid solutions to those who are suffering from debilitating diseases which have afflicted humankind for centuries. We met these demons head on and we have uncovered some real answers for you.

In this book, you'll learn about a potential cure for arthritis. You'll learn how to practically eliminate your chances of getting heart disease or cancer. We take on Alzheimer's. We take on psoriasis. We take on chronic fatigue and depression. We take on the misery of asthma and allergies -- we face up to all the big ones and provide you with down-to-earth ways to take action!

We'll show you how to get free prescription drugs, or a way to buy your drugs at a dramatically reduced price. We'll show you a natural way to get to sleep at night without the use of drugs. We'll provide you with excellent remedies for that aching back of yours, and much more.

The Most Valuable Book Ever Written helps you to stop being a victim and to fight back, whether it be a medical condition or a persistent financial problem.

Speaking of finances, do you want to learn a new and innovative way to start saving money today for your retirement, without putting a crunch on your cash flow today? In this book, you'll find a detailed way to do just that. Do you want to purchase the automobile of your dreams and a price so low you never thought it could be possible? This book will show you how to do just that. Are you tired of being pushed around by insurance companies? Do you need health insurance that you can afford? Well, just about everything you need to know about the confusing world of insurance is "de-mystified" for you within these pages.

But this book is about more than just problems. It's about the fun, thrill and enjoyment of life, and how you can more of all of it.

What to dramatically improve your chances of winning the lottery? We think we've uncovered to excellent tips on how to do just that. Want to turn your favorite hobby into a business that could make you rich? You can! We'll show you how. Here's an exciting idea: more or retire to an exciting, comfortable foreign country and live the life of your dreams. There are many ways that it can be done easily. Have you written a book that you think has a chance of being a best seller if only you can get it past the editors and get it published? You'll find some excellent advice on how to do just that in this book.

You can use this book however you want to. If you are not interested in any particular topic just now, you can start on Page 1 and just start reading. This book is designed to engage your mind and get you thinking about possibilities you might never have thought of before.

You can skim through it and stop at those headlines or section heads that catch your eye or attention. If you have a specific problem, you're likely to find something in this book that will either provide you with direct answers, or lead you to where you can find what you need.

This is the kind of book that can provide you with hours upon hours of absorbing, interesting reading. It's the kind of book that make you want to nudge your partner in the side and say, "Hey! Did you know...!"

It's nearly impossible that you won't learn something new from this book. It's impossible that this book will not pay for itself many times over. It's impossible that this book will not put more money in your pocket. It's impossible that this book will not do something to make you healthier, or teach you a new and exciting way to have fun, and just plain get more out of life.

If it didn't do all of these things, then it couldn't live up to its name: *The Most Valuable Book Ever Written!*

Medical Miracles

ALLERGIES DON'T HAVE TO BE MISERABLE

It is a beautiful Saturday morning in mid-June and you decide to mow the lawn. As you pull your lawn mower out of the garage, your neighbor, George, drops by to chat for awhile. You are in the middle of stating your strong opinions about your favorite baseball team's recent slump, when a dreaded thing happens—you have an itchy feeling in your throat and nose, and your eyes begin to water like Niagara Falls. You try to get yourself under control, but before you know it you lose control—you sneeze explosively at George, not once but several times. You feel terribly embarrassed, but there is no way of controlling your reaction. The allergy season has arrived to haunt you for another season.

An allergy occurs when your body is exposed to something it doesn't like. Your immune system mistakenly identifies a particular substance around you as something potentially dangerous and sends antibodies to the rescue. The antibodies trigger the release of histamine and other defensive chemicals. These, in turn, cause the itching sneezing, tears and fatigue you experience during an allergic reaction.

If you suffer from some form of allergy, you are not alone. Allergies affect between 35 and 50 million Americans every year. The most common form of allergy is hay fever, which is a reaction to some form of pollen in the atmosphere. However, you can be allergic to almost anything, from food and fur to insects and Christmas trees.

Don't despair! No matter how bad your allergic reaction is, there are things you can do to make your environment a little easier to live in. Below are some of the more common allergies along some suggestions on how to control them.

AIRBORNE ALLERGIES

• Keep your grass cut short. If you can, find someone to mow it for you. If you have to work outside, cover your nose and mouth with a mask that can act like a filter. A mask also works indoors if you need to vacuum your rug and you are allergic to dust and dust mites.

• Don't dry your clothes outside. Pollen collects in the cloth fibers and can make your allergy unavoidable. At the same time, you do want to wash your clothes and bathe frequently to reduce the amount of pollen you collect when traveling from one place to another.

• Stay indoors when the pollen count is high, and avoid walking or exercising in parks, gardens, and woods. The best times to run errands is after a rain or in the late afternoon.

• Ban smoking in your surrounding environment. It can only aggravate an allergy. Other irritants to avoid during allergy season include alcohol, perfumes, hair spray,bug spray, chlorine, and laundry detergent fragrances.

• Plan your vacation with your allergies in mind. You might ask your doctor to suggest a place where the source of your allergy isn't pollinating during your vacation. Also, don't move just to avoid your allergies. Chances are, once you settle in, you may develop an allergy to something in your new environment.

•Keep your house, furniture, and car clean. In your car, you can keep the interior dust-free by vacuuming carpets, upholstery, and the heater and air-conditioning vents. It also helps to vacuum your furniture upholstery weekly, and wash all your bedding in very hot water at least once a week to kill dust mites.

• You might love your carpeting and your beautiful velvet drapes, but chances are they are contributing to your allergies. Heavy drapes, rugs, wool blankets, down bedding, and overstuffed chairs are great dust collectors and make cozy little homes for dust mites. Your best bet is to remove all the carpets from those rooms in which you spend the most time, like the bedroom. (Now is a great time to install that lovely parquet wood floor you've had your eye on all these months!) Also, get rid of the heavy drapes and overstuffed furniture and replace them with light curtains, window shades, and washable slipcovers. In the bedroom, use airtight plastic mattress and pillow covers, and cover the heater vents with cheesecloth to help screen out particles.

• Keep the windows closed whenever possible and use an air conditioner in the summer. You should also acquire a dehumidifier to cut down on mold spores, if mold is a problem for you.

I mentioned dust mites several times because they are powerful little creatures who make the lives of many people miserable. Dust mites are microscopic cousins of ticks and spiders that live in our carpets and furniture. However, they do not bite like ticks and spiders. The items which make people allergic to dust mites are the bodies of dead mites and feces left behind by the little critters in their wanderings.

Dust mites haven't always been a problem. Before the introductions of conveniences like the vacuum cleaner and central heating, people kept most of their homes too cool for the mites, and throw rugs were used instead of carpets. Today, houses are warm and most carpets don't get the vigorous cleaning once given to throw rugs.

PETS

With dogs and cats, the allergies arise primarily from the animals' dander. The most logical way to avoid pet allergies is to not keep an animal around the house, unless it doesn't have fur and dander, like a fish. But for a lot of people, it is easier to suffer with an allergy than to give up the love of a special animal friend. Here are some tips on how to keep your pet and get rid of the allergy:

• Bathe the animal at least once a week. Even cats can get a bath, and some kitties learn to enjoy bathing in the sink after a time. The key is patience.

• Keep your furry pets away from any rooms you frequent a great deal, especially bedrooms. Their dander can accumulate in the fibers of your carpet or your favorite chair and make your life that much more miserable. You may notice that you continue sneezing even after you begin to frequently wash your pet. This is because of the animal dander that still remains in your rugs, drapes, and furniture.

• Clean your house, especially those areas where the pet spends most of its time.

• Don't use any product which has down as an ingredient. Down pillows, comforters, and jackets are warm and cozy, but they can cause as much of an allergic reaction as dogs and cats.

INSECTS

Of all the allergies, insect allergies are potentially the most deadly. Some people have such severe reactions to bee or fire ant stings that they can go into shock and die. People with severe reactions usually get a bee sting kit from their doctor which allows them to administer an antidote immediately after being bitten. But even if you aren't really allergic to insect bites, it is no fun getting stung. There are many things you can do to avoid insect bites.

• Don't walk around outside without shoes on. Nothing can compare to the burning, fiery pain of stepping on a honeybee barefooted.

• Keep tabs on any hives, nests and ant mounds in your yard. Your safest bet is not only to avoid them, but just get rid of them. If you have to, hire an exterminator.

• Wear neutral-colored clothes, like white or tan, while outside. You might be mistaken for a flower, if you wear bright blue, yellow, orange, or red.

• Don't cook meals, feed your dog, or paint outside. These activities have odors which might attract insects.

• Don't use perfumed products when you know you will be spending some time outdoors. This means avoid hair spray, suntan lotions, and certain kinds of makeup.

Sometimes you have no idea what makes you sneeze and wheeze. You've thoroughly cleaned your house, bought a state-of-the-art air filter, and banished poor Fido to the back yard, and still your sinuses run. Your best bet is to make an appointment with a professional allergist. The allergist will put you through a series of tests to determine what it is that makes you react in your environment.

Some people use antihistamine and decongestants to control their allergies. Over-the-counter antihistamine can leave you feeling drowsy. If you want to take this medication and stay alert, see if you can get a prescription for nonsedating antihistamine from your doctor. Decongestant can work to reduce the plugged-up feeling in your nose, but their effects are usually only temporary. One way to relieve congestion and rinse the allergy-causing material from your nose is to rinse your nasal passages with a mild saltwater solution.

Occasionally, people decide to do away with their allergies completely through treatments. If you've had enough of your allergy, you can try taking shots to get rid of it. The idea behind the treatment is to introduce the material to which you are allergic into your bloodstream over a long period of time. This gives your body time to build up an immunity to your allergen. When administered correctly, the shot treatment can be very effective.

A CHEAP WAY TO AVOID EXERCISE-INDUCED ASTHMA

These days, many people work hard to maintain a good level of physical fitness. They run, swim, do aerobic dancing, or participate in a combination of activities which makes them feel healthier, happier, and more relaxed.

But if you have asthma, physical exercise can be anything but comfortable. Often, an asthma attack occurs in the middle of exercising—making you wheeze and gasp for air, and cutting your activities short. Asthma sufferers usually turn to their medications when attacks occur, but the medicine can cause heart palpitations in some people, and others simply do not like using the inhalers which dispense the medication.

Recent research indicates that there is a much simpler way for asthmatics to avoid attacks while exercising. By wearing a surgical mask during physical activities, asthmatics cut back as much as 100 percent on the number of attacks suffered.

The surgical masks are made from compressed fiber material. They decrease asthma attacks by preventing moisture and heat loss during rapid breathing. Usually, it's that loss of heat and moisture which brings on the asthma attack during exercise.

The mask might help as many as 10 to 12 million people, or three-quarters of the U.S. population of asthmatics, enjoy the healthful benefits of exercise without fear of recurring asthma attacks.

THE LATEST ON ALZHEIMER'S

When Alzheimer's disease strikes a member of your family, it can be one of the most wrenching things that happens. Your loved one not only gradually loses his memory, but also loses the ability to communicate and control physical functions, and weight loss can be significant. In the past, doctors couldn't do much for patients who contracted the disease. Although there is still no cure for Alzheimer's, researchers have made some very important discoveries which may lead to prevention, early detection, and perhaps an eventual cure for this dreaded disease of the mind.

The Alzheimer's Home Test

Perhaps you have noticed that Grandpa seems to be not quite the same as he once was. He has difficulty remembering even things as simple as the fact you wanted him to get a loaf of bread at the store. If you are concerned that he is developing Alzheimer's disease, there is a simple test Grandpa can take at home which reliably shows if Alzheimer's is present.

Ask Grandpa to draw the face of a clock on a piece of paper. If he draws a clock which looks perfectly normal, probably the only thing wrong with him is he suffers from a little short-term memory loss—something which happens to everyone as they get older. If, however, the clock he draws looks like a piece of modern art, with the numbers out of sequence, the chances are good that Grandpa has Alzheimer's. This test is based on the idea that Alzheimer's disease affects long- as well as short-term memory and the idea of a clock is stored in a person's long-term memory.

Another thing to look for at home is noticeable weight loss, even though Grandpa might be eating his normal amount of food. Research indicates this weight loss might be caused by an increased metabolism in Alzheimer's patients.

The Gene

Dr. Allen D. Roses of Duke University recently discovered that a rather common human gene might contribute to the likelihood of a person developing Alzheimer's. The gene makes a protein called apolipoprotein E (ApoE). In the past, researchers believed this protein's only job was to move cholesterol in and out of cells and tissues. Dr. Roses' experiments indicate that ApoE might also move a substance into the brain which destroys memory over time.

The substance, beta amyloid, is a gooey, glue-like material found in the brains of Alzheimer victims. The amyloids appear to create holes in brain-cell membranes which allow deadly levels of calcium to enter and destroy the cells.   Dr. Roses' research shows that certain Alzheimer patients have a form of ApoE which binds with the beta amyloid found in the bloodstream and deposits it in the brain. Although everyone is born with ApoE, not everyone has the Alzheimer creating ApoE. Whether you develop Alzheimer's disease or not depends on what form of ApoE you inherited.

Dr. Roses' studies open the door for future developments in the war against Alzheimer's disease. In the future, doctors may be able to run tests early in a person's life to determine if he or she has the "wrong" kind of ApoE. Perhaps scientists will create a medication which prevents ApoE from picking up the beta amyloids, thereby at least reducing the chances of someone getting Alzheimer's. Although no exact proof exists that this disease is caused by a gene you inherited from your parents, at least it is a step in the right direction toward understanding and curing Alzheimer's.

Nutritional Deficiencies

Although there isn't anything you can do to choose which gene you inherit, research indicates you can reduce your chances of developing Alzheimer's disease by watching what you eat. Elderly Americans especially seem to have a difficult time eating properly to get the right nutrients.

One of the important nutrient deficiencies associated with Alzheimer's is magnesium. Studies show a lack of magnesium may make you more at risk for Alzheimer's. A magnesium deficiency can come from not eating enough of it in your diet, the use of many sorts of drugs (which is common among the elderly), and a change in the way your body processes food. Another potential problem is a lack of vitamin B-12. A B-12 deficiency can cause your brain and memory to work less efficiently. If you have any questions about nutritional deficiencies, talk to your doctor.

Aluminum

Another possible contributor to Alzheimer's disease is mankind's increased intake of aluminum. Aluminum enters your body by your eating plants and animals which have been exposed to it. Research indicates that aluminum might stimulate the manufacture of free radicals, or toxic particles, in your body. These free radicals accumulate in the brain, causing you to slowly lose control of your brain functions. Based on this theory, one possible cure for Alzheimer's disease is the use of antioxidants to break down the free radicals.

You can control your intake of aluminum by avoiding foods which are high in the mineral. One example of aluminum carrying food is fish and seafood. Although not all fish contain the harmful mineral, some have been exposed to aluminum because of the water in which they live. If possible, find out where your fish came from before you eat it.

Stay Mentally Active

The old "use it or lose it" principle still exists! Recent studies show that the more you use your brain, the less likely you are to develop Alzheimer's disease. So, whatever you do, don't let yourself fall into a rut, especially after retirement.

Read books, take classes, visit new places, meet new people, develop new hobbies—do things which are different and that you think you might enjoy. You might surprise yourself at how much happier and healthier you feel after you break away from the routine of watching television all day, every day. Just get out and enjoy your life!

ARTHRITIS PAIN IS AVOIDABLE

Arthritis is probably one of the more painful long-term diseases a person can experience. Probably you either have some form of arthritis now or you know someone who does. Although people still manage to get around with this disease which destroys the cartilage between the bone, the pain and crippling caused by arthritis can greatly reduce the quality of your life.

The good news is you don't have to suffer with arthritis. If you don't already have it, there are ways to avoid developing osteoarthritis, that final stage of arthritis where the cartilage is completely gone and bone grates against bone. If you have arthritis, you might be interested to discover that there is a little known cure on the market which not only stops cartilage destruction, but can also help rebuild cartilage. Either way, you can avoid at least some of the pain and inconvenience of arthritis.

Six Steps to Avoiding Arthritis

The real trick to keeping arthritis out of your life is to be careful with your body:

• Eat a well-balanced diet.

• Keep off the excess weight. It takes a lot of extra effort for your body to maneuver around extra weight.

• Do warm-up exercises before getting seriously involved in sports and strenuous activities. This prevents you from putting unnecessary stress on your muscles and joints.

• Try not to overuse your joints. If there is an easier way to accomplish something, by all means do it!

• When you work, use tools which put as little stress on your joints as possible. This might be as simple as using a wheelbarrow to move dirt instead of buckets, or as complicated as acquiring the latest computer keyboard which does away with the normal flat keyboard in the interest of saving your fingers and wrists.

• Wear shoes that fit well and support your ankles, knees, and back. This means saying good-bye to spiked three-inch heels, which are horribly uncomfortable anyway! There are plenty of good-looking shoes on the market which fit this criterion.

Glucosamine Sulfate: A Miracle Cure?

If you already have arthritis, there is still hope for you. It comes in capsule form and is called glucosamine sulfate. Unlike the painkillers—aspirin, Motrin, Naprosyn, Feldene, Clinoril, Vicodine, Meclomen, and Indocin, among others—glucosamine is a totally safe and natural remedy. Although U.S. doctors are more inclined to treat the pain rather than try to cure the disease, European doctors have done research which shows the effectiveness of glucosamine.

In order to reverse the cartilage destroying effects of arthritis, the body has to produce connective tissue, which is the primary ingredient of cartilage. The first step in creating connective tissue is the body's conversion of glucose to glucosamine. When found in high concentrations in the space between the joints, glucosamine sulfate stimulates the production of connective tissue. The connective tissue then acts as a buffer between the bone joints and prevents the grinding and the pain of osteoarthritis.

One of the research projects put together by European doctors included a comparison study between glucosamine and a commonly prescribed arthritic drug, Motrin. Dr. Antonio Lopez Vaz of Oporto, Portugal gave one group of arthritis patients 1.5 grams of glucosamine daily, and another group 1.2 grams of Motrin. During an eight-week period, the group receiving the Motrin at first felt a lessening of pain, but by the eighth week, their pain was returning. The glucosamine group experienced a lot of pain during the first two weeks, but week eight ended with the glucosamine group feeling a lot less pain than the Motrin group.

Another problem with the painkilling drugs generally prescribed by doctors is the chance of toxicity. This is especially true in the case of Indocin, which is 1,000 to 4,000 times more toxic than the non-toxic glucosamine. When you consider the long period of time it takes to go through arthritis therapy and the amount of toxicity which can build up in your body, researchers consider glucosamine to be 10 to 30 times better than treatment with a powerful drug like Indocin.

Glucosamine sulfate can be found in health food stores. The manufacturer, Enzymatic Therapy, of Green Bay, Wisconsin, produces it in 500 milligram capsules known as GS-500. Call the manufacturer at 414-469-1313 for the name of a health food store near you that carries glucosamine. Sixty capsules cost about $20. The normal dosage is three to four capsules a day for at least six weeks. If you experience a lot of pain, use four to six capsules.

The important thing is to consult your doctor, especially if you are presently on any kind of anti-inflammatory medication. If possible, move away from the painkillers during a trial period with glucosamine sulfate.

Also, don't forget to exercise and eat a nutritionally balanced diet to help you maintain a healthy body and attitude. With the help of your doctor and a natural cure, you just might be able to beat the agony of arthritis!

BACK PROBLEMS: HOW TO AVOIDTHEM

Back pain can come on so suddenly, you might not even know what you did to cause it. Perhaps you exercised too long, or that sofa you tried to lift was too heavy. Maybe you slept in the wrong position last night, or you bent over too long while gardening. Whatever the cause, backaches can really put an end to all physical activities. If you are normally a very active person, a back problem can be irritating, as well as painful.

The good news is you don't have to suffer from backaches. There are several easy ways to both avoid back trouble and to cure it once it happens.

Avoid a Bad Back

A backache usually indicates that you probably pulled some muscles or ligaments in your back. The best way to avoid the pain is to baby your back—make sure it gets plenty of exercise, but try to prevent the occurrence of any excess strain.

• Don't sleep on your stomach. Although this might feel very comfortable as you drift off, sleeping on your stomach puts a lot of extra pressure on the natural curves of your spine. The best way to rest is either on your back with a pillow under your knees or on your side with a pillow between your knees.

• If your job requires long periods of standing, say at a cash register or on an assembly line, you can help avoid back pain by putting a telephone book, a stool, or a small box under one foot. This helps to relieve some of the strain on the small of your back. Also, if possible, slowly stretch and touch the floor every half hour to get rid of added pressure on your back muscles.

• If you have a choice, when moving a heavy object, push it instead of pulling it. By pushing, you let your legs and body weight do the work instead of your back.

• When you lift a heavy object, bend from the knees instead of from the waist. Once again, this lets your legs do the work instead of your back.

• Sometimes your bed is the back pain culprit. If your mattress sags in the middle, and you can't afford a new one, put a piece of plywood between the mattress and the box spring to give your bed added support. Another alternative is to buy a more expensive mattress with greater support.

Get Rid of That Pain!

• If you strain your back, the best thing you can do is just sit or lie down for awhile. By doing so, you give your back a chance to rest and heal. However, you don't want to stay in bed forever, just for a day or two. The longer you stay in bed, the harder it is to get your body back into the swing of things.

• Put an ice or a heat pack on your back. Ice reduces swelling and back strain, while heat can relieve muscle spasms. Or use both, if they both help you to feel better.

• Find someone who can give you a back rub. It doesn't have to be a vigorous, spine-snapping back rub, just some firm pressure where the muscles are the most tense. This can drive away the pain, makes your back more supple, and it can be very relaxing.

Although you don't have to do it right away, there are times when you should see a doctor. These include times when the pain lasts for more than two days without letting up; back pain that extends down into your leg or foot; and back pain which is accompanied by a fever, chest pains, stomach cramps, or difficulty breathing. Remember, there may be more wrong with you than just your back. Sometimes back pain is just one symptom of a more serious problem.

CATARACTS: YOU CAN PREVENT THEM

Cataracts, a disease in which a cloudiness develops in the lens of the eye, are one of the major illnesses in this country today. Nearly 40,000 people are blind from cataracts, and over four million Americans have substantially impaired vision. Removal of cataracts is one of the leading causes of surgery, with almost 500,000 people undergoing cataract surgery every year.

However, you can prevent, or even reverse cataracts, by improving your nutrition and by using nutritional supplements— namely vitamins and minerals. This is because the main cause of cataracts are substances known as free radicals. Free radicals are toxic particles which are present in our diet and are generated by our bodies through the usual process of metabolism. They collect on the eye's lens and scar the tissue to where you can no longer see out.

Nutrition and Supplements

Some of your cataract prevention can be introduced through your diet. You need a daily supply of 800 units of vitamin E, 5,000 milligrams of vitamin C, 15,000 units of beta carotene, and 30 milligrams of zinc, along with sulfur-containing amino acids like cysteine, glycine, and glutamic acid. There are also antioxidants present in a green salad filled with raw vegetables. In other words, by eating properly, which you should be doing anyway, and taking some vitamin supplements, you can avoid cataract formation.

One of the most interesting ingredients in this anti-cataract recipe is vitamin C. The lens of the eye contains the highest concentration of C than anywhere else in the body, so an increased amount of vitamin C helps protect your eyes. Studies show that eyes with cataracts have no vitamin C present in their lenses.

Doctors who have experimented with the use of diet to control cataracts have had some pretty good results. With patients who already have cataracts, but who adjusted their diet, 65 percent experienced improved vision and 50 percent avoided surgery completely.

Ocudyne

If you already have cataracts, a further ingredient available to you is the antioxidant formula of Ocudyne. The Allergy Research Group created this supplement to improve lens nutrition, and it contains some of the necessary sulfur-containing amino acids. You can get 200 capsules of Ocudyne from the Group for $35.95 plus $3.50 for shipping by calling 800-782-4724 or 510-639-4572.

Sunglasses

The most amazing thing about sunglasses is that you don't need them to protect your eyes from the supposedly harmful ultraviolet (UV) light. Of course, wearing a pair of sunglasses in high glare situations is nice. However, research indicates UV light might protect your eyes from cataracts. This conclusion is based on the fact that people who live in the mountains or the deserts in the Southwest, where UV rays are at higher levels, have fewer incidences of cataracts than people who live on the East Coast, where there is more cloud cover.

Another indication that UV light is all right for your eyes is the existence of all the animals on earth. Most animals spend much of their time in direct sunlight, but they rarely contract cataracts.

Like the animals, you, too, can improve your cataracts or avoid getting cataracts altogether! Simply eat a nutritious diet high in antioxidants and go to your eye doctor on a regular basis for a check-up, and you should be able to see well for a long time to come.

SAVE ON PRESCRIPTION DRUGS

Once upon a time, getting a doctor's prescription filled was as simple as going down to your neighborhood drug store and having Hal, the friendly pharmacist, fill it. Hal knew everything about your family's health, from what kinds of prescription drugs you've taken in the past, to which summer little Junior had the measles. Hal's word on drugs and health was as good as gold, superseded only by the doctor. And you didn't mind paying a bit more for your drugs to get the comfort of familiarity.

Things have changed dramatically today. Not only are there more and more prescription drugs on the market, but they seem to cost more every year. If you take a drug over an extended period of time, or if you need several prescriptions at once, you need to find the cheapest source. The good news is you are no longer tied down to Hal and his drug store for all your prescriptions. He might have a great price on some drugs, but chances are you can get other drugs cheaper elsewhere. The following is a list of alternatives which you might want to check out to save yourself money on your prescriptions.

Generic Substitutions

This option applies only to drugs which have lost their original patent. Of the top 50 sellers, 26 drugs have lost their patent. The first generics on the market usually cost at least 30 percent less than the original brand name. As other drug companies begin making their own versions of a drug, the price spirals down. A good example of this is the common antibiotic amoxicillin. One hundred 250-milligram tablets of amoxicillin cost around $7.88. The same amount of the same drug dispensed under its brand-name Amoxil costs $21.60.

When you get generic drugs, you might notice that they don't look like your usual brand-name drugs. That is all right. The U.S. Food and Drug Administration allows companies to trademark the specific shape and color of their pills. The actual ingredients will still be identical, as will their rate of absorption into the body.

Some states allow pharmacists to exchange generic drugs for brand-names without the doctor's permission, unless the physician specifically ordered no substitution on the prescription. You can ask your pharmacist about your state's rules.

Occasionally, there are drugs which should not be substituted. Among these drugs are those that regulate heart rhythm, control epilepsy, and replace thyroid hormones. Generics aren't recommended for these health problems because even a tiny difference in absorption rate might be dangerous. If you need to have your blood tested regularly to make sure the drug level stays the same in your body, you probably shouldn't buy a generic version.

Therapeutic Substitution

When you get a therapeutic substitution, you switch to a different, cheaper member of the same class of drug, like switching one beta-blocker for another. Although the drugs may be different, this substitution is possible because they have identical clinical effects. A great example of therapeutic substitution occurs among the non-steroidal, anti-inflammatory drugs (NSAIDs), which are used to treat arthritis. Sometimes over-the-counter aspirin can be just as effective as the much more expensive NSAIDs.

Besides NSAIDs, other drugs which are good candidates for substitution are blood-pressure medications, ulcer drugs, and birth-control pills. Because you are exchanging two separate drugs with the same effects instead of accepting a cheaper version of the same drug, it is extremely important to ask your doctor whether therapeutic substitution is right for you.

Comparison Shopping

You probably shop more than one grocery store looking for the cheapest prices for your favorite fruits and cereals. Why not be just as careful getting your prescriptions filled? By calling around, you might discover one pharmacy charges much less for your needed drug than another. The differences in prices usually reflect different overhead costs. Some pharmacies also lower the prices of their most popular products to bring customers into their stores.

Your best bet is to call different pharmacies for each drug you need, because no pharmacy is consistently cheaper. Another thing you need to do if you comparison shop is to keep track of each drug's usage. If you get prescriptions refilled more often than normal, it might signal a worsening of your problem.

Mail-Order Pharmacies

American Association of Retired Persons
800 456-2277
Family Pharmaceuticals
800 922-3444

Hospitals

Sometimes you can buy drugs from a hospital pharmacy, if you are under the care of a hospital-based doctor or being treated at a hospital clinic. The discounts hospital normally receive can be passed on to you, giving you a substantial savings. For instance, an oral morphine compound used during cancer treatment can cost $26.40 at a hospital and $102.20 at a local pharmacy.

Manufacturer Aid Programs

Most major drug companies have programs now which give free drugs to people who have no insurance and no way to pay for the drug out of pocket.

Usually, this program is geared toward people with very low incomes, but if your drug is very expensive, even for a middle-class income, you might be eligible.

The pharmaceutical companies only accept applications from physicians, not from individual patients. If your doctor needs more information on the program, he or she can call the Pharmaceutical Manufacturers Association and ask for a guide to these programs.

The Brown Bag Review

This is particularly important if you take a number of different drugs, as many elderly people do. When you have a brown bag review, you put all your medications into a brown paper bag and take them in to your doctor for identification. Sometimes the review may indicate you are taking too much medicine, or different medicines which conflict with one another.

Often people go on taking a drug even when they no longer need it, especially if the drug is habit-forming like the tranquilizer Valium. The doctor can point out the medications you no longer need, thereby decreasing the number of drugs you need and saving you money.

SOLVE YOUR CHRONIC FATIGUE PROBLEMS

We've all experienced it at sometime or other—that feeling of mental and physical tiredness; the desire to stretch out on our desks in the middle of the afternoon and take a snooze; the knowledge that no matter how many cups of coffee we drink in the morning, the day will be gone before we accomplish anything. These feelings are a result of chronic fatigue.

Millions of Americans, especially women, complain about chronic fatigue every year. Although it is not a disease, fatigue can lower your productivity at work and at home. The very best way to combat fatigue is to exercise, eat right and get plenty of rest. However, there are other things you can do to give yourself more energy. They are:

• Listen to classical music, tapes of nature sounds, gospel, or pop music. By listening to these sounds, you can slow your pulse and lower your blood pressure. One of the primary sources for chronic fatigue is stress. As you relax while listening to music, you get a new lease on life, and you will probably get up from your chair ready to tackle the world.

• Do deep breathing exercises. You might be surprised to notice that sometimes when you feel most fatigued, you breathing actually becomes shallow. This can rob your body of necessary oxygen it needs to run at peak efficiency.

Deep breathing exercises consist of laying on your back with your knees pulled up and your feet slightly apart. As you inhale through your nose, relax your stomach and concentrate on pulling the air into your abdomen. Then breathe out through your nose and imagine your lungs and abdomen collapsing as the air leaves. Repeat the exercise 10 times.

• Take a warm bath, or use a hot tub with whirlpool jets to help relax your muscles. Studies show warm water stimulates brain waves related to deep sleep. You will probably get a good night's sleep, thereby defeating fatigue before it can rear its ugly head.

• Schedule an extra 15 minutes every morning to pull yourself together. A little early morning relaxation means you won't feel as rushed and tired the rest of the day.

• Start your day with a plan and a set of goals. If you know what you want to accomplish, the number of things you need to get done won't seem so overwhelming. Make a list of what you need to do, figure out what's most important, and work to get it done.

• Shut off the boob tube. Watching television is a passive activity. It can rob your brain and body of crucial energy you might need for a more important task. If you need entertainment, read a good book. Interacting with a book and its characters will stimulate your brain and give you more energy.

• Work out your problems. Whether you have difficulties at home or at work, do your best to solve them. Apologize to your husband or wife, have a good conversation with your son, ask the boss for that larger desk you've always wanted. Do whatever it takes to solve your problem. A great deal of energy can go down the drain while you stew about something other than your job.

• Stop smoking. Smoking robs your body of vital oxygen and decreases your energy levels.

• Try not to oversleep. Getting too much sleep can leave you groggy and cranky for the rest of the day. Most people can usually get by with six to eight hours of sleep.

• And finally, a fun way to battle fatigue—take a vacation. Simply getting away from the problems and ruts of your job can be invigorating and might give you a new lease on life. At the very least, you can return from your holiday refreshed and with a positive attitude. If fatigue is a major problem for you day after day and week after week, make sure to schedule a check-up with your doctor. Such a long bout with fatigue might mean there is something seriously wrong with your body. Fatigue is a symptom of illnesses like diabetes, lung disease and cancer. It might also mean that you simply need a break in your routine, like an all-expense paid trip to Bermuda. That would certainly be a prescription worth filling!

CURE YOUR INSOMNIA

Everyone has had trouble falling asleep at some time or other in their lives. Whether the inability to sleep is caused by starting a new job, or moving to a new school, or some other disruption in your life, when it happens day after day it can seem as if you will never get another good night's sleep as long as you live.

Now there is some hope for the chronic insomniac in the form of a lollipop-shaped device that fits in the mouth of the troubled sleeper. The treatment, called low-energy emission therapy (LEET), uses the device, a spoon-shaped antenna, to emit harmless electromagnetic waves which help people fall asleep. The antenna is connected to a box which produces the electromagnetic waves. Researchers believe the electromagnetic waves block sleep-preventing chemicals in the brain. In tests done on insomniacs, 80 percent who used LEET fell asleep faster and slept longer than insomniacs who did not receive the treatment.

LEET has no side effects, which makes it better than the more traditional sleeping pills prescribed by a physician. One side effect of pills is they can cause worse insomnia after the effects wear off or after the patient stops taking them. Another good aspect about LEET is that the patient can fall asleep with the antenna in his mouth without worrying about choking on the device. The antenna is too large to be swallowed, and it shuts off a few minutes after the patient falls asleep.

The one drawback to LEET is it doesn't work for everyone. The best candidates for the treatment are people who suffer from recurring stress. It doesn't work for patients whose insomnia is caused by psychiatric disturbances or medical disorders.

The treatment, after FDA approval, will be available by prescription and will cost around $100. It can mean a good night's sleep for millions of stressed-out Americans.

A NEW CURE FOR PSORIASIS

For those of you who periodically suffer from that itchy skin condition known as psoriasis, there is new hope for you. Researchers have discovered that a form of vitamin D, called D-3, helps control, and possibly even cures psoriasis.

What is psoriasis?

Psoriasis occurs when skin cells accelerate the amount of time it takes to mature and shed. Normal skin cell take about a month to go through the process, but with psoriasis the process speeds up to three or four days. Because the skin cells divide faster than normal, a thick patch of dead cells accumulate on the surface of your skin. An attack of psoriasis can last for weeks or months.

Vitamin D-3

Research done at Mayo Clinic in Rochester, Minnesota shows that two preparations of vitamin D-3, when used in ointment form, improves patches of psoriasis within eight weeks. The scientists also experimented with taking vitamin D-3 orally, but it is less effective this way. Vitamin D-3, when taken orally, can alter your body's calcium metabolism.

In order to work, vitamin D-3 ointment needs to be at a strength available only by prescription. Over-the-counter vitamin D pills and creams do not work against psoriasis. The D-3 ointments are already available in Europe and Canada, and will be ready for prescribing in the U.S. in a year or two, pending Food and Drug Administration approval.

Other treatments

At the present time, Americans with psoriasis have three options for controlling the condition—self-therapy, phototherapy, and medications. Right now, there is no known cure for psoriasis.

SELF-CARE: If you have mild psoriasis, a daily warm bath with mild soap can soak off the excess cells. Try to keep your skin moist with emollient creams, but avoid using a cream containing lanolin which might make your skin more sensitive.

For your scalp, use shampoos like Head & Shoulders, Zincon, Exsel, Selsun, or Capitrol. You might need to work up a lather and leave it on your head for at least five minutes to get the best results.

You can also buy over-the-counter salicylic acid or coal-tar soaps, lotions, creams, and ointments. Or your doctor might prescribe a drug especially suited to your condition.

PHOTOTHERAPY: Phototherapy means taking advantage ultraviolet radiation to cure psoriasis. On your own, you can try exposing your skin to moderate amounts of sunlight, which might improve some patches. However, try not to burn yourself, since a sunburn can make psoriasis worse.

Usually a doctor will prescribe phototherapy if you suffer psoriasis on 30 to 50 percent of your body. Phototherapy in a medical setting uses ultraviolet B radiation, ultraviolet A radiation, and a combination of light sensitizing medications.

MEDICATIONS: The most severe cases of psoriasis receive medications. The most prescribed drugs are corticosteroid creams, Anthralin, Cyclosporine, Methotrexate, and Etretinate. However, the majority of these drugs have some less than desirable side effects. For example, corticosteroid creams work, but long-term usage can cause your skin to get thinner, changes in the pigment of your skin, and the psoriasis patches rapidly return after you stop applying the cream.

Anthralin is a good drug for large patches of skin, but it can stain your hair, skin, and clothing and may irritate normal skin. Cyclosporine, which is usually used to prevent organ rejection, was recently approved to combat severe psoriasis. There are no known side effects to date. Methotrexate, an anti-cancer drug, and Etretinate, a form of vitamin A, are both used orally to treat severe form of psoriasis. These two drugs, however, have liver toxicity among their side effects. When you have psoriasis, it is a tough decision—should you take drugs or use smelly, messy soaps or just hope that it eventually goes away? No treatment is perfect, and nothing cures the condition. Hopefully, the FDA will soon allow vitamin D-3 ointments on the market. If you suffer from psoriasis, perhaps this is the cure for you.

HOW TO AVOID HEART DISEASE

One of the facts of our times is that no matter how advanced our science and medicine has become, heart disease remains one of the major killers of Americans today. Nearly one out of every two deaths is due to diseases of the heart and blood vessels. What is even more tragic is many cases of heart disease can be controlled or avoided altogether by paying attention to your lifestyle. There are several things you can do to decrease your chances of heart disease.

If someone in your family is already a candidate for a heart attack, you need to be prepared ahead of time. If the unthinkable actually happens and your loved one is actually struck down with a heart attack, it pays to know ahead of schedule how to handle the situation. Here are some tips on what to do if a member of your family is a candidate for a heart attack.

• Talk to your doctor.
Before a heart attack even occurs, discuss different treatments with your doctor, especially the latest treatment which involves clot-dissolving drugs that can halt a heart attack if administered quickly. Find out from your doctor if your loved one is a candidate for this treatment.

By putting together a plan of action before you need it, you can save valuable time in an emergency. Also, you may be too panicked during the attack to think clearly, so it pays to already have the major decisions out of the way.

• Choose a good hospital.
Ask your doctor to help you choose a hospital which regularly uses clot-dissolvers or which specializes in heart attack treatment. It also helps if the hospital's emergency room is known for its fast response time.

• Always carry medical information.
Make sure you always have an updated copy of your family member's medical information in your wallet. This information should include:
√ The names of your physician and a back-up physician.
√ A brief family medical history.
√ A list of medications currently being taken.
√ A list of any allergies or past reactions to drugs.
√ A photocopy of the electrocardiogram (EKG).
√ A letter from your doctor which says your loved one has been successfully evaluated for clot-dissolving therapies.

When you already have this information available, the treatments can begin that much sooner, perhaps saving your loved one's life.
• When your family member actually has a heart attack, one of the best things you can do is know the warning signs.
They are:
√ Pain or pressure in the center of the chest which lasts for at least two minutes.
√ Pain that spreads to the shoulders, neck, or arms.
√ Shortness of breath.
√ Dizziness or nausea.

If your family member experiences these symptoms, call 911 immediately, or get your loved one to a hospital as soon as possible. Don't let your family member argue with you and tell you it is just heartburn or a gas attack which will go away soon. Many people have died waiting for the pain of a heart attack to go away.

• Unless your doctor advises against it, give your loved one an aspirin. It will help prevent blood clots from forming and can save his life until emergency personnel arrive.

• At the hospital, call in a cardiologist for a second opinion, if you aren't completely satisfied with the initial diagnosis.

• Get advice from your doctor on how to care for your loved one. He will be affected both physically and mentally by the heart attack, and will need a lot of extra support.

• Encourage your heart attack victim to adopt a healthier lifestyle. If he wasn't receptive to the idea before the attack, he might be now. Of course, the best way to avoid a heart attack is to take some preventative measures. By eating right, exercising, and watching your blood pressure and cholesterol, you can go a long way toward protecting yourself from future heart problems.

HYPERTENSION

Hypertension is a term used to indicate an abnormally high blood pressure in your arteries. When the pressure of the blood on your arteries is very high even without the added pressure of the heart pumping, it can lead to a bad situation. It is a serious problem because high blood pressure is one of the leading causes of heart disease and strokes.

When you get your blood pressure taken at a clinic or doctor's office, the nurse writes down the result as a fraction. The upper and higher number of that fraction is the systolic pressure, which indicates the blood pressure when the heart is beating. The lower number indicates the blood pressure between heart beats. If the diastolic reading is unusually high, the diagnosis is hypertension.

Normal blood pressure has a diastolic reading of less than 85. When you have high-normal blood pressure, the diastolic reading is between 85 and 89. If your diastolic reading is between 90 and 104, you have mild-high blood pressure.

Before you can be diagnosed with hypertension, you doctor needs to take several blood pressure readings to establish a pattern of high blood pressure, since readings can be influenced by many things, including the position of your body; your age; the time of day; whether or not you recently exercised; and your intake of drugs like caffeine, nicotine, and alcohol.

The level of your hypertension determines what kind of treatment your doctor prescribes. Doctors often prescribe hypertension medication for people with mild-high diastolic blood pressures. If you have a prescription for medication, make sure you ask your doctor about potential side-effects. Many drugs used to control hypertension have side-effects which range from headaches and fatigue to nausea, dizziness, and impotence. For people with mild cases of hypertension, often changes in lifestyle are all that is needed to bring the high blood pressure under control.

If you are diagnosed as having high blood pressure, you are not alone. Approximately one-fourth, or 65 million Americans, have hypertension. Of that number, 75 percent have mild cases of hypertension. For 95 percent of the people suffering with hypertension, there is no known cause. However, there are risk factors which can play an important role in the level of hypertension from which you suffer.

• Risk factors.

Of all the risk factors which can contribute to the seriousness of hypertension, only one is beyond your control. You can adjust the other risk factors to help bring your diastolic blood pressure reading within normal range. The risk factors include:

√ Genetics

Genetics is the primary risk factor for hypertension. Although you can't change the genes you were born with, you can use your family's medical history to your own advantage. If you know that your grandparents and parents all had hypertension and died of strokes or heart disease, you will be doing yourself a favor by paying attention to your blood pressure and reducing your other risk factors.

√ Weight

Your weight can be a second risk factor. When you are overweight, you put more stress on your heart and blood vessels. Twenty to 30 percent of all people with hypertension can benefit from losing weight, and may be able to get by without any medications.

√ Alcohol

People tend to overlook the effects alcohol can have on blood pressure. If you are a social drinker, which means you have three to six drinks during the course of the day, and you have hypertension, consider giving up the drinking and see what it does for your blood pressure.

√ Exercise

Exercise can be a wonderful, healthy way to reduce high blood pressure. If you exercise three or four times a week, you can only do your heart good. But you can get too much of even a great thing. Excessive amounts of exercise are not good for you and may even increase your blood pressure, as you body compensates for all the work by raising the pressure.

√ Sodium

Studies go both ways on the subject of sodium intake. Some researchers say there is little evidence which suggests that sodium is a contributing factor in hypertension. However, most researchers agree that there is an obvious relationship between how much salt you eat and how high your blood pressure is.

To be on the safe side, it can only help to cut back on how much salt you eat. The American Heart Association's recently set limits on sodium intake. The association says you should restrict sodium intake to one gram per 1,000, and don't exceed three grams a day.

√ Stress

Few researchers doubt that stress can contribute high blood pressure. What isn't agreed upon in the scientific community is the effectiveness of stress reduction techniques, like biofeedback meditation.

It appears that meditation alone does not permanently reduce hypertension. In fact, the benefits of biofeedback meditation on high blood pressure do not seem to last beyond the meditation session.

Biofeedback meditation is a relaxation method—it is not a miraculous cure for hypertension. The only way meditation works well on hypertension is if you meditate in conjunction with other doctor recommended anti-hypertensive therapy. In other words, don't throw your pills away just because someone tells you meditation is the answer to all your problems. Get your doctor's permission before making any major changes in your therapy.

√ About smoking

Believe it or not, research indicates that smoking has no effect on hypertension. If you stop smoking tomorrow, you blood pressure will go neither up nor down.

But this doesn't mean that you get away scott-free by smoking. The studies also indicate that, like hypertension, smoking is an independent risk factor for heart attacks. If you have hypertension and smoke, you at least double your risk of heart attack.

CHOLESTEROL

Like hypertension, high levels of the wrong kind of cholesterol is a primary cause of heart disease. There is actually a total of three kinds of cholesterol, and they are classified according to their density.

The first, very low density lipoproteins (VLDL), is composed primarily of triglycerides. The second type of cholesterol, low density lipoproteins (LDL), contains high amounts of cholesterol. The third kind of cholesterol is high density lipoproteins (HDL), which has a high concentration of protein.

Because proteins in the blood act as carriers for triglycerides and cholesterol, you want to encourage the presence of HDL cholesterol in your blood stream. Although no one is sure about exactly what HDL does, a popular theory suggests that HDL picks up cholesterol from the walls of your arteries and transports it to your liver for transportation from your body.

The other two forms of cholesterol, VLDL and LDL, act the opposite way. They help to deposit cholesterol in your artery walls. Without enough HDL to carry away the extra cholesterol, all this extra material, or plaque, builds up on your artery walls until the blood flow is radically slowed or stopped. You then have a condition known as atherosclerosis.

Usually, this plaque builds up in the arteries around your heart. A heart attack occurs when a blood clot gets caught in a clogged artery whose opening is too small to allow passage of larger items in the blood stream.

· Ways to reduce "bad" cholesterol levels

Reducing your bad cholesterol level requires a many pronged attack plan. As in the case of hypertension, you need to exercise and reduce your levels of stress. You should also get plenty of rest and quit smoking. A person who has high cholesterol and smokes has a 236 percent risk of having a heart attack. If you smoke, have a high cholesterol level, and hypertension, your chances of a heart attack jump to 384 percent!

Your primary method of attacking high levels of bad cholesterol, however, is to change your diet and get rid of excess fat in your meals. Most people recommend cutting your intake of fat back to 20 to 30 percent of your entire caloric intake.

One problem with this is that you may never lose your desire for fatty foods, so every meal can become a struggle to keep your fat intake under control. If you don't trust your willpower, your other alternative is to drop your fat intake all the way down to 10 percent.

Eating fatty foods also affects your level of alertness. When fat gets into your bloodstream, it makes your red blood cells sticky enough to clump together. These "clumps" move slowly through you circulatory system, clogging up capillaries as they go. Clogged capillaries means your brain does not receive all the oxygen it needs, which results in a feeling of grogginess. When you eat a low-fat diet, there is nothing in your blood stream to clump together your red blood cells, and you end up feeling more awake and alert after meals.

· The 10 percent fat diet

A 10 percent fat diet doesn't mean you give up all the good things in life—it merely means you are more careful about your food choices. Instead of broiled chicken, baked potato with sour cream, peas in a cream sauce, and a nice dish of ice cream, all of which total 55 grams of fat, you eat baked skinless chicken, baked potato with nonfat sour cream, steamed peas, and a tasty dish of frozen yogurt. This second menu contains just nine grams of fat—you automatically saved yourself 46 grams of fat!

It may sound difficult at first to get used to a 10 percent fat diet, but as the weeks go by, the foods you used to like, such as hamburgers, french fries, and potato chips, will begin to taste too greasy. An added bonus is the weight you will lose because your body will no longer have to store all that excess fat.

If you decide to use the 10 percent diet, your foods should fall within three categories—those you eat all the time, foods you can eat occasionally, and stuff you wouldn't touch with a 10-foot pole.

√ The foods you can eat all the time are:
* Lean meats, especially fish and fowl.
* Egg whites.
* Cereals which contain no fat, sugar, or salt.
* Tofu and other soy products.
* Pastas made without oil or eggs.
* Nonfat dairy products.
* All fruits, fruit juices, and vegetables, except olives and avocados, which contain too much fat.
* Peas, beans, lentils, and other legumes.

√ **The foods you can eat occasionally are:**
* Smoked or charbroiled food, because they contain a potent carcinogen.
* Low-sodium soy sauce.
* Pastas made with eggs.
* Sugar, molasses, sucrose, and other sweeteners.
* Caffeinated drinks, but no more than two cups a day.
* Breads and cereals made with added fats.
* Lobster, crab, and shrimp, all of which have quite a lot of cholesterol.
* Olive oil or canola oil, if used sparingly.
* Low-fat (one-percent) dairy products.

√ **The foods you should never eat are:**
* Fried foods.
* Egg yolks.
* Salt or salty foods.

* Meat fat, margarine, butter, lard, and hydrogenated vegetable oils.
* Mayonnaise.
* All nuts, except chestnuts.
* Fatty meats, such as organs, cold cuts, and most cuts of beef and pork. Also avoid chicken skin, which is almost pure fat.
* Nondairy creamers and any other source of palm or coconut oils.
* Polyunsaturated fat, such as corn oil and most other vegetable oils.
* Whole dairy products, like whole milk, cream, and sour cream.

The way to figure out how much total fat is in your diet is to multiply your total daily intake of fat (in grams) by nine, which is the number of calories per gram of fat. Next, you divide this number by your total daily calorie intake. You will probably have to keep a journal of the fat and calorie content of each food you eat. Eventually, however, you will automatically learn to judge which foods are best for you.

· The 10 percent fat diet is not for everyone

While many people can get by on the 10 percent diet, it is not for everyone. Certain people can even be harmed by having too little fat in their system. Let's use a documented case as an example.

A middle-aged man stayed on a very low-fat diet for eight years. In that time, he lived mostly on steamed vegetables and skinless chicken. However, despite his diet, the cholesterol levels in his blood stream remained high.

After a series of tests, his doctor discovered that this man's very low-fat diet completely screwed up his metabolism. Instead of accepting the diet, his body responded like it was starving. His liver started producing more bad cholesterol and his levels of triglycerides, the main component of VLDL cholesterol, were very high.

The man could only bring his body back under control by adding additional fat to his diet, until his daily levels of fat intake rose from around 10 percent to about 25 percent.

The moral of this story—do not start a diet, especially a

very low-fat diet without the consent and recommendations of your doctor.

MORE WAYS TO FIGHT HEART DISEASE PROBLEMS

Although nothing can take the place of the advice already given for protecting yourself against heart disease, you might consider some other ways listed below of reducing your chances of dying from heart disease. They are:

· Vesnarinone

Vesnarinone is a drug specifically aimed at the more than three million American patients who suffer from congestive heart failure. When you suffer from congestive heart failure, your heart muscle is weakened because of a heart attack or some other cause.

As the disease gets progressively worse, you may find yourself getting short-winded or fatigued after doing even the smallest chore, like bringing a sack of groceries from the car into the house. Between 30 and 50 percent of all people diagnosed with this disease die within a year of diagnosis. Only 20 percent of patients with congestive heart failure live beyond five years after diagnosis.

Vesnarinone, when used in combination with other drugs, allows the heart pump better, improves irregular heart rhythms, and dilates blood vessels, allowing more blood to reach the heart. Of the nearly 500 people who received the drug so far, the rate of death dropped 62 percent. During this study, the only noticeable side-effect was a decrease in white blood cells which raised the risk of infection for a small number of patients. Vesnarinone will be available by prescription, pending approval from the Food and Drug Administration.

· Instant coffee—protection against heart disease?

According to a study done on over 10,000 Scotch men and women, instant coffee may help protect against the risk of heart disease. In the study, nearly 22 percent of the subjects showed signs of having heart disease.

Even after blood pressure, smoking, and cholesterol were taken into account, the people who did not drink coffee had a significantly higher prevalence of heart disease than coffee drinkers.

These results are opposite from results received from Scandinavian countries. However, one major difference between the cultures is that Scandinavians like strong, boiled coffee, while in Great Britain the people prefer instant coffee.

· **Foods which regulate the circulatory system.**

In certain cases, using food to control and prevent heart disease can go beyond cutting fat from your diet. For example, a glass of red wine at meal times can reduce your chances of blood clotting problems, because red wine is full of blood thinners from grape skins.

One food which might be helpful in lowering your blood pressure is celery. This old Vietnamese remedy contains a pressure-lowering chemical. Finally, cholesterol can be lowered by eating beans, walnuts, and oats. One-half cup of cooked beans a day can reduce your level of cholesterol by as much as 10 percent.

Heart disease is not something you can simply brush aside. With so many people dying from it every year, you need to pay attention to your own health. By eating right, exercising, reducing stress in your life, and having regular check-ups to make sure your blood pressure and cholesterol levels are normal, you can go a long way toward avoiding heart disease.

All of this may seem like too much of a bother, but ask yourself this—which is easier, doing something healthy for your body, or planning a funeral?

CURE THAT SNORING!

Here it is, three a.m., and the orchestra serenades you again. It happens every night at this time, and frankly you've had enough. As the crescendo rises in the room, you would like nothing more than to get your largest frying pan out of the kitchen and bop your husband on the head the very next time he opens his mouth and snores. However, before you resort to violence, take heart! Doctors have discovered a new, fairly inexpensive way to cure snoring forever!

The Cure

The procedure, called laser-assisted uvula palatoplasty (LAUP), is performed in a doctor's office. Unlike the more expensive and more involved surgeries of the past, LAUP takes only about 15 minutes and allows the patient to get back to normal life immediately.

With LAUP, the doctor injects the back of the patient's mouth with novocaine. The doctor then uses a laser to trim and reshape the palate and the soft tissue which hangs from the palate. Because the palate and soft tissue causes the snoring by blocking airflow through the air passages, this procedure solves the problem. To date, LAUP has a 90 percent rate of cure.

For many people, LAUP is effective after one treatment, but some people may need three or four treatments. The total cost for LAUP is about $2,000. Prior to the development of LAUP, chronic snorers were treated to major surgery—general anesthesia, hospitalization, and a long recovery—for about $10,000-$12,000.

If you are interested in the LAUP procedure and want the name of a doctor in your area who performs it, call Dr. Jack Coleman at 615-322-6366.

Other Methods

Even if you do not want to spend $2,000 to get rid of a snoring problem, there are still a few other methods you can use without getting out the frying pan or banishing the snorer to the next county.

• Try losing some weight. Just being a little overweight can create a snoring problem, and the more obese you are, the more likely you are to snore.

• Don't have a nightcap. Drinking alcohol before bed can make snoring even worse.

• Stop smoking. Most smokers snore.

• Get rid of your pillow. It might take some time to get used to sleeping with your head flat on the bed, but pillows put a kink in your neck which can increase snoring.

• Buy a pair of ear plugs. This method is directed at the long-suffering spouse. No one has yet invented a plug for the snorer's nose and mouth.

THE LATEST HELP FOR VARICOSE VEINS

Varicose veins are a hereditary disease which affects the veins in the legs. Along with the bluish, swollen veins and the red "spider veins" come tired, aching legs for the sufferer. And the sufferers are plentiful—17 percent of the population inherited the varicose vein gene, most of them women.

Varicose veins occur when the tiny valves inside the leg veins are damaged. Because the blood cannot move efficiently through the vein and back to the heart, it pools and the vein bulges from the strain. Unfortunately, varicose veins are more than simply a cosmetic problem—they can become a serious medical problem if a blood clot forms in a vein, or if a vein ruptures and leads to excessive bleeding. If you have a blood clot or a rupture, see your doctor immediately.

Most varicose veins do not end up medical emergencies, but everyone who suffers from them would love to get rid of them. If you do not want to go through with the hospitalization and expense of cosmetic surgery to remove the veins, researchers have developed a more inexpensive way to have varicose veins removed.

Echosclerotherapy

The new procedure, called echosclerotherapy, is done in the doctor's office, and people who receive the treatment are free to resume all normal activities immediately. Because it doesn't require hospitalization, echosclerotherapy is a lot less expensive than regular surgery.

The doctor begins the procedure by using an ultrasound machine to find the deep veins which feed the varicose veins. He then inserts a tiny tube into a surface vein and pushes it through until it reaches the feeder vein. The doctor uses the tube to inject a harmless iodine solution into the vein. The varicose vein collapses and is eventually absorbed into the body. So far, the treatment works about 80 percent of the time, and the only side effect is mild temporary inflammation in the treated leg.

If you are interested in echosclerotherapy and want to find a doctor who performs it, call the North American Society of Phlebology at 619-632-5990.

Lessen the Pain

While you decide whether or not to try echosclerotherapy, there are a few home procedures you can use to lessen the pain and tiredness in your legs.

• Prop your feet up. When you stand for long periods, gravity works against you and pools the blood in your varicose veins. By propping your feet up higher than your hips, you give the blood a chance to move out of your legs and return to your heart. Sometimes it helps to lay on the floor with your legs straight and your feet propped against a wall for a few minutes.

• Wear support hose. You can usually buy support hose in a drug or department store. The hose can really help your legs feel better by preventing the blood from pooling and instead moving it back into the deep veins for the return trip to the heart.

When you have an especially crippling case of varicose veins, buy a pair of elastic stockings from a medical supply store. Elastic stockings work on the same principle as support hose, only much more so. Don't just buy any elastic stocking—you need to be fitted for a pair to insure a proper fit.

• Wear a good pair of low-heeled, comfortable shoes. Avoid high heels and cowboy boots like the plague.

• If you smoke, stop. Research indicates smoking may be a risk factor for people with varicose veins.

• Get some exercise. The best thing you can do for your poor legs is take them for a walk, especially if you have been standing or sitting for a long time. A little walking throughout the day helps prevent the blood from pooling.

To recap—rest, exercise, hosiery, and common sense can help you control the aching and tiredness in your legs brought on by varicose veins. And if you get tired of the veins or they become too much to handle, see a doctor about having them removed.

Tips on Reducing Your Stress

Stress and worry, worry and stress-whether we like it or not, we all experience them at sometime or other during our lives. We feel stress about taking a test, and if we didn't study, our worries about failure take over our lives. When we go on vacation, the change in normal routines can cause a great deal of stress, and sometimes we worry that we aren't having as good a time as we should. We even worry when we feel stress, because we know it can lead to high blood pressure, heart disease, and cancer.

A little stress or worry is a normal part of life. However, if you think fretting about things is taking up way too much time and effort, you need to work at bringing your life back under control. The following are some easy tips on how to control your stress and worries and take charge of your life once again.

• Take a look at past worries.

By analyzing your past worries, you can not only see what bothered you, you also discover how you handled them. For example, say you had a great many worries about money in the past. When you analyze this worry, you find you handled the problem by setting up a family budget and sticking to it. The fact that you actually solved a worry in the past can be a great confidence booster—it means you can do it again.

• Decide how you will handle your worries.

Sit down and make a list of all the things you are worried about. Then try to figure out solutions for all your worries and list those, too. You now have in front of you a plan of action, which puts the ball back in your court. Knowing that there really are solutions makes you feel less helpless and undecided.

• Talk to someone you trust.
By keeping your worries to yourself, you can easily blow your concerns way out of proportion. Discussing your worries with someone gets a load off of your chest and makes you feel better. And who knows? Maybe the other person can put things in their proper perspective and offer some good solutions.

• Convert a negative into a positive.
When you have a problem you're worried about, two alternatives exist. You can look at the problem negatively and never try to attack or solve it, or you can use your worry as a positive spring board into something better.

For instance, when you know a test is coming, you can either worry yourself sick about failing, never get around to studying because you are sure you'll fail anyway, and then it becomes a self-fulfilling prophesy. The other option is using the time you might have spent worrying to study. Or perhaps there is someone in your office who is getting all the praise and credit from the boss. You might handle it by feeling envious and by worrying that you will lose your job to that so-and-so. Or you can work harder at your own job with the knowledge that it will probably pay off for you in the future.

• Try to think of the worst thing that can happen.
Say you were fired, what would you do? You would go on interviews and find another job. Maybe you would start your own business. The important thing is to figure out how to handle the worst. Once you have the worst under control, anything less won't seem as bad.

• Act, don't wait.
The longer you wait, the worse the problem can become, and the more you end up worrying. If you have a pain in your stomach that won't go away, simply worrying about it isn't going to help at all—it might make the situation worse. You need to see a doctor immediately, because it could be something serious.

• Distract yourself.

When you find yourself worrying, focus your attention elsewhere. Watch TV, talk to a friend, or read.

• Seek counseling.
Sometimes worries actually do become too much to handle. If you see no way out of your concerns, try seeking help from a professional therapist or joining a support group.

Another way of dealing with your stress and worries involves letting your body move into a state of deep relaxation. This method of stress reduction is harmless, inexpensive, and in no way requires you to join a religious cult. Called transcendental meditation, the procedure gives you a technique for achieving an altered, relaxed state of consciousness.

When you meditate, you choose a word or sound, called a mantra, which you repeat over and over in your mind. By concentrating on a single item, you empty your brain of the distractions which were raising your stress levels. Moving away from those distractions gives your body a chance to slow down, calm down, and eventually relax.

Medical research shows meditation lowers your blood pressure, which makes it a very good practice for people with heart disease, hypertension, or high cholesterol levels. The best thing about meditation is that it is much easier to handle a problem in a calm state of mind than when you are stressed out.

The Procedure

For 10 to 20 minutes twice a day or when you feel a need, do these three things:

1) Take several long, slow, deep breaths to relax.

2) Focus on the muscular tension in your body and relax these muscles completely by thinking of them as warm, heavy and comfortable.

3) Select a comfortable mantra—a word, phrase, or sound—and start repeating it over and over in your mind. You should almost immediately feel a discharge of tension and experience a state of

relaxation which will increase as you continue meditating.

When you finish the exercise you will feel fresh, rejuvenated, and ready to take on the world. What is more, you will be in control, not your stress.

DRUGS THAT ENHANCE SEX

Sometimes, as people get older, their sexual abilities decrease. Either they have less desire for physical love, or the desire is present, but the body doesn't respond too well. If you feel your sex life could stand improvement, there are drugs available which might give you the help you need. They are:

ELDEPRYL—Some doctors consider this a wonder drug. By protecting the levels of the neurotransmitter dopamine in your brain, Eldepryl automatically enhances your sexual function, along with improving your memory, motivation, and physical energy. Eldepryl is currently used mainly as a treatment for Parkinson's Disease, but more doctors are prescribing it to patients who are primarily interested in its sexual potency qualities.

One 61-year-old patient took Eldepryl to enhance his sexual function. Almost immediately, his frequency of sexual activity increased from once a month to 18 times in 17 days!

A main drawback to Eldepryl is that one pill usually costs around two dollars. However, for non-Parkinson's patients, the dosage is usually so low that it becomes quite affordable.

YOHIMBINE—This drug helps impotent men by stimulating the sympathetic nervous system, which controls the erection of the penis. Although it is not 100 percent effective for everyone, studies show that up to 45 percent of the men taking Yohimbine were at least helped. Some of the patients actually returned to full potency.

The side-effects of this inexpensive little pill include feelings of nervousness and a slight increase in blood pressure, but no serious side-effects have been reported.

NIACIN (VITAMIN B3)—Unlike the two previous drugs, niacin is a non-prescription substance. By taking 50 to 150 milligrams of niacin 15 to 30 minutes before sexual activity, the niacin enhances the sexual flush, stimulates vaginal lubrication, and may increase the intensity of the orgasm.

Talk to your doctor for further information on these or other drugs available which might increase your sexual potency.

FIVE MINUTES A DAY TO A THINNER YOU

Do you have the slight bulge around the middle which is just noticeable enough to keep you out of the pants' size you want to wear? Are you too busy to spend an hour a day at the gym using someone else's professional equipment?

If you answered yes to either of these questions, there is still hope. With just five minutes a day, you can perform the following exercises which are geared toward flattening your bulging abdomen and getting you back into your clothes.

Waist toner

Stand with your knees bent and your feet about shoulder-length apart. While keeping your back straight, clasp your hands behind your head with your elbows pointed out. Keeping your stomach muscles tight, exhale deeply and bend sideways to the left from your waist as far as you can. Return to your original position and exhale. Next repeat the procedure while bending as far as possible to the right. Return to the center and repeat the exercise for a full minute, keeping your breath regular and even.

Tummy tightener

Lie on your back with your knees bent and your right foot on the floor. Put your left ankle on your right knee. Clasp your hands behind your head and keep your elbows back. Bring your shoulders and head off the floor about four inches, using your stomach muscles only. Hold your position to a count of 10 and then slowly lower your head back to the floor. Switch legs and repeat the procedure. Do it two times on each side.

Sleeker sides

Lie on your back with your left ankle resting on your right thigh. Put your right hand behind your head. Slowly raise your head and shoulders from the floor and twist to the left from your waist while counting to three. Slowly lower your head to the floor. Switch sides and repeat exercise. Do it five times on each side.

Rock your tummy away

Lie on your back with your knees bent and your feet flat on the floor. Keep your arms resting at your sides on the floor with your palms turned down. Bring your knees up into your chest, while pulling your buttocks off of the floor. Use your stomach muscles to do the work. Repeat the exercise 10 times, bringing your knees as close to your chest as possible.

These exercises can be done anytime you have five minutes to concentrate on your abdomen, whether between meetings at the office or at home while watching your favorite program. Also, the procedures described here do not put the excessive strain on your back the way regular sit-ups do.

BEAT THOSE MOODY BLUES!

Kate E. was 29-years-old when it struck her. She had just married a terrific guy, moved to a new city, and started working in an exciting new career with a West Coast firm. Everything seemed to be going perfectly for her—but something was definitely wrong. She woke up in the morning feeling more exhausted than when she went to bed. Kate found it hard to concentrate on her work and it became impossible to meet deadlines. Kate's husband noticed the difference also, because she began to withdraw from him and all her friends. Socializing became painfully exhausting as it became harder to concentrate on conversations among her friends.

Kate E. had a classic case of what everyone knows as "the blues."

The blues, or depression, can happen to you as a result of a number of causes. Sometimes depression arises from a major change in your life, like what Kate E. experienced in the example above. In a short period of time, Kate changed her lifestyle, moved, and started a new career—any one of which can be overwhelming to the average person.

The blues can also be a result of a lack of change—a seemingly deadened job which shows no promise for future advancement. A lack of exposure to sunlight, especially in late winter, can also trigger a bout with mild depression. Even the pills you take can influence your moods. One thing to realize—almost everyone feels sad or low at some point in their lives. You are not alone.

Take a Look at Your Pills

If you feel blue, especially for more than a day or two, and you can't understand why, take a look at your prescriptions. Depression can result when you start, change, or stop using certain medications. It is important to know which drugs carry depression as a side effect. Below is a list of prescription drugs which may cause depression. The brand name of each drug is followed by its generic name in parentheses. If you are taking one of these drugs and feel unusually depressed, see your doctor immediately.

HIGH BLOOD PRESSURE DRUGS—Aldomet (methyldopa), Catapres (clonidine hydrochloride), Combipres (chlorathalidone and clonidine), Lopressor (metroprolol), Raudixin (rauwolfia serpentina), Serapsil (reserpine), Tenex (guanfacine).

ESTROGEN TAKEN FOR MENOPAUSE SYMPTOMS—The generic drug diethylstilbestrol, Estinyl (ethinyl estradiol), Estrace & Esteraderm (estradiol), Estrovis (quinestrol), Ogen (estropipate), Premarin (conjugated estrogens), Tace (chlorotrianisene.

TOPICAL ESTROGENS USED FOR VAGINAL DRYNESS—D.E.S. (diethylstilbestrol), Estrace (estradiol micronized), Ogen Vaginal Cream (estropipate), Ortho Dienestrol Cream (dienestrol).

INSOMNIA AND ANXIETY DRUGS—Ativan (lorazepam), Centrax (prazepam), Dalmane (flurzepam), Libritabs & Librium (chlordiazepoxide hydrochloride), Restoril (temazepam), Serax (oxazepam), Tranxene (chlorazepate dipotassium), Valium, Valrelease (diazepam), Xanax (alprazolam).

NAUSEA MEDICATIONS—Librax (clidinium bromide and chlorodiazepoxide hydrochloride), Reglan (metoclopramide).

PARKINSON'S DISEASE DRUGS—Symadine & Symmetrel (amantadine), which are also antiviral agents; Dopar, Larodopa & Sinemet (levodopa).

OTHERS—Epitol & Tegretol (carbamazepine), used as anti-convulsants and anti-neuralgics; Haldol (haloperidol), a tranquilizer; Inderal & Ipran (propranolol hydrochloride), fights angina, arrythmia, hypertension and migraine; Indocin (indomethacin) an analgesic and anti-inflammatory; Procamide, Procan, Pronestyl (procainamide), used for arrythmia.

SAD

SAD is more than just a description of a state of mind—it is an actual condition called seasonal affective disorder. Studies show that women are four times as likely to be affected by SAD than men. Seasonal affective disorder occurs when you are particularly sensitive to different amounts of daylight. It usually strikes during the winter when there are fewer hours of sunlight and disappears with the coming of spring.

SAD is more than just the traditional "cabin fever," a feeling that if you don't get out of the house soon, you will begin shredding the wallpaper and curtains one square inch at a time. With SAD, you find that you lack the energy you had not too long ago; you feel more like sleeping than normal; and no matter what happens, you can't shake the blues.

If you believe you might suffer from SAD, there are a number of things you can do to make life easier. The most imporant thing is to talk to your doctor. He or she can make some suggestions which can help. You can also try introducing more light into your environment. Increase the number and quality of lights in your working and living spaces. Arrange to take a walk outdoors frequently, especially when the weather is decent and sunny. Take up an outdoor activity like cross-country skiing, which is not only good exercise but almost guarantees you will be soaking up precious light. If you have to and can afford it, take a trip to a sunnier part of the country when life back home gets particularly dreary. Winter can get miserable, but it doesn't have to drag you down!

Why Women More Than Men?

Women are much more likely to be affected by the blues at sometime in their lives than men are. Part of the reason for this are hormones and the differences between male and female brain anatomy. Actually, until children reach puberty, the boys are more likely to feel some symptoms of depression. However, once the hormones start roaring, it is the girls who are more likely to show moodiness and to feel mild depression.

However, other things also create the separation of the sexes when it comes to depression. For one thing, starting with puberty, girls feel a lot more pressure to measure up to society's standards than boys do. When a girl doesn't quite look as thin as the model on the cover of her favorite magazine, she may have feelings of inadequecy and depression. This response to society's standards can carry over into adulthood as women are told they can juggle a family, a house, and a career, but find instead that their juggling act is a great deal tougher than it sounds.

Depression can also arise within the workplace. Women might find that their career aspirations are taken less seriously than the plans of their fellow male workers. A working woman might find herself passed over for a promotion or excluded from a better job because of her gender. This can cause feelings of remorse and self-recrimination, leading to a bout with depression.

What Can You Do About Depression?

You don't have to just sit there and suffer and hope the feelings of sadness go away! There are several things you can do to relieve, or at least lessen, the blues. One way to handle depression is to seek professional help from a trained therapist. Whether you go to a therapist or not, the first step to beating depression is pinpointing the source of your feelings. For Kate E. at the beginning of this chapter, the source of her blues was all the major, if positive, changes she made in a short period of time.

If you cannot afford a therapist, at least find someone—a relative, friend, teacher, or pastor—with whom you can talk about your feelings and problems. If talking about your problems makes you cry, then CRY! Crying can be a tremendous emotional release and you will probably feel better afterward.

Another way to decrease mild depression is to pick an activity you enjoyed doing before you became depressed, and then do it. You can also exercise or do some other physical activity, like visit a friend or volunteer your time to some organization. The important thing is to GET OUT OF THE HOUSE! Mild depression only deepens if you sit around your house moping and feeling isolated.

Do not try to make any major decisions while you feel depressed. If you decide to buy a brand new fire engine red BMW with white leather seats because you think it might make you feel better, chances are when the bill arrives you will fall back into your depression. In fact, stay out of malls and department stores altogether when you feel depressed. Buying new items might cheer you up for awhile, but not if you overextend your credit.

Also, avoid eating binges, especially when they involve pizza, cookies, and gallons of ice cream. Eating will make you feel better for a time, but your next trip to the bathroom scale might catapult you back into your blue state.

Remember, almost everyone feels sad and blue at some time in their lives. Sadness is a part of life. Although it might seem as if it will last forever, mild depression won't if you talk to someone about it and don't let it take over your life.

HOW TO LOOK YOUR MOST YOUTHFUL

What is the worst thing that can happen to a woman? Imagine for a moment that you are invited to a party to meet your husband's new boss. Because this is an important occasion, you take some care to look your best. As you apply your makeup in the bathroom mirror, you take stock in your appearance. You don't look bad with long, straight hair—after all that's the way you've worn it for years—and you feel the gray streaks make you look distinguished. So there are a few wrinkles around the eyes and mouth—they show the world you like to laugh a lot. You gained a few pounds after the birth of your third child, but still you don't look too bad. There is still a hint of a shape under your bulky sweater. A few finishing touches and you are ready for the party.

When you get to the party, everything seems just right. You know just about everyone, the food looks good, and the music is right. Everything is perfect—until you meet the new boss. Somehow, during the introductions, the new boss mistakes you for your husband's mother! If you could melt through the floor to China, you would at this moment.

Unfortunately, stories like this really happen. Whether or not you look 10 years older than you really are, the important thing to remember is YOU DON'T HAVE TO LOOK OLD! No matter what your age, in one year you can shed 10 years from your appearance simply by using the following common sense guidelines:

Get Fit

Many of the things which are part of your normal routine can be converted into ways to burn calories and lose weight.

• Whenever possible, stand instead of sitting, because standing uses up more calories.

• Use the stairs instead of the elevator. When you are healthy, stair climbing not only burns calories, but it also strengthens your lungs and heart, as well as tightens your leg muscles and your buttocks.

• Don't park right next to the building you work in or the main entrance to the mall. By parking further away, you force yourself to walk the extra distance, thereby getting even more exercise.

• Take a short walk four times a day to burn calories and stay alert.

• Maintain an active sex life. Sex uses up calories and makes you look and feel younger.

• Exercise for 30 minutes three times a week. This doesn't have to be a grueling workout. Choose something you enjoy doing, like jogging through the park, swimming, or cross-country skiing. If you don't like doing your exercise, there is a 99 percent chance that you will trash the whole idea of an exercise program within a month.

• Wear a comfortable pair of running or walking shoes. When shoes hurt your feet, they end up making you look and feel years older.

• Stand up tall and straight. Good posture makes you look taller, slimmer, younger, and more confidant.

Eat Right

• Get rid of the extra weight, especially if you are still carrying around baby fat from your third pregnancy and your baby is now in school. However, don't buy into the latest crash diet fad. Instead, slowly switch to a low-fat diet which allows you to lose a pound a week. Low-fat means lowering your fat intake to about 30 percent of your food per day.

• A low-fat diet doesn't mean you have to suffer. You can fill up on fresh fruits and vegetables, especially if you succeed in eating five servings of fruits and vegetables a day. These foods give your body the vitamins it needs to fight aging.

• You can also indulge on a low-fat diet by eating low-fat snacks, like air-popped popcorn and rice cakes.

• Make sure you get plenty of calcium from low-fat dairy products to maintain strong bones and a youthful posture.

• Cut back any alcohol intake to one or two drinks a day. Alcohol is a source for empty calories and dehydrates the skin.

• Also slow down your caffeine intake to one cup of coffee or tea or one can of soda a day. Without the caffeine, you will appear much calmer and not so stressed out.

• Put away the salty foods. Salt makes your body retain water and makes you look bloated and fat.

Stay Beautiful

• Get rid of puffy eyes every morning by washing your face in cold water. It also helps to dampen a washcloth with ice cold water and hold it to your eyes for a few minutes. If neither of these techniques works, moisten tea bags in cold water and hold them to your closed eyes for two minutes.

• To prevent your hair from getting dried out and limp-looking, wash your hair with products that contain a sunscreen and wear a hat outdoors.

• Find a flattering hair style. You would be surprised what a change in hair style will do for your looks and your personality. If you have problems with gray hair, dye it a shade of color that works well with your skin tone.

• If your hair is naturally thin, add body and volume to it by getting a gentle perm.

• Get plenty of sleep. Most people require at least seven hours per night. Without sleep, you end up pale-skinned and with dark circles under your eyes.

• Brighten your smile by using a nonabrasive tooth polish and schedule regular checkups with your dentist.

• To get rid of dry skin on your elbows and knees, apply baby oil to them weekly before you bathe. Then rub baking soda into the oiled areas. After your bath, rub your elbows and knees with moisturizer.

• On sunny days, wear a good pair of sunglasses to prevent you from squinting.

• Because the sun's radiation can damage your skin and cause wrinkles, use plenty of sunscreen on any exposed parts.

• Drink at least eight glasses of water a day. Water helps keep the skin clear and healthy looking.

• If you smoke—STOP! Smoking dries out the skin and makes it look like leather. A 40-year-old woman with a two-pack-a-day habit can easily end up looking like an 80-year-old grandmother without half trying.

Any one of the above suggestions can help you look and feel younger. Taken together, they can lead to a healthier, happier lifestyle—a lifestyle which leaves no room for being mistaken for your husband's mother.

TOXIC CHEMICALS IN YOUR HOME

When you buy store items like bug spray or varnish remover, it's natural to assume that they are potentially dangerous. After all, they smell bad and give you a headache if you are around them for awhile. Chances are you leave a window open in the room in which you are using the bug spray or varnish remover. Probably you arrange for your young children to be out of the room or the house while you are using the products so the youngsters don't have to breathe the fumes.

But what about the other products in your house? How safe are the cleaners, furniture polishes, and floor waxes you probably use every week?

According to recent studies, inhaling fumes from a variety of cleaning, painting, and home repair products can affect the nervous and respiratory systems, the liver, kidneys, and heart if exposure occurs over a long period of time. Laboratory tests have shown that long-term exposure can also cause cancer in laboratory rats and humans.

The ingredients in these products which cause the problems are the organic solvents. Manufacturers put these solvents in their products to help clean grease and dirt, or to make sure that the products stay in the same condition in which they were packaged—liquids remain liquids, solids stay solid.

The thing to be concerned about when using these products is the fumes. Most products print a warning on their labels informing potential users that inhaling the fumes may be harmful. If you feel drowsy, intoxicated, disoriented, or have a headache while working with a product, you've had too much exposure to the product's fumes.

People with heart or lung disease and pregnant women should try to avoid exposure to solvent fumes. When you work with solvents, there are several things you can do to decrease the dangers of breathing harmful fumes. They are:

• Read the label and follow any directions. If you aren't willing to do what the product says, don't buy the product.

• Check to make sure there isn't another product on the market which you can use that contains smaller amounts of solvents.

• Don't use more than one product containing solvents at a time, and don't use one right after another.

• Don't drink alcohol while working with a solvent. It might seem like a great idea to have a few beers while stripping the varnish off of a piece of furniture, but alcohol can increase the solvent's toxic effects. If you are taking medication, ask your doctor whether it is safe to use a solvent.

• Use a fan in your work area to help break up the fumes. If the directions tell you to wear a respirator, gloves, or goggles, buy them.

• Because fumes sometimes sink instead of rising in air, be careful about receiving even more vapors as you bend over your work.

• Keep all solvents out of the reach of children, and keep children out of work areas where solvent fumes are present.

Some of the more common solvents listed in the package ingredients include methylene chloride; toluene; 1,1,1 trichloroethane; glycol ethers; n-hexane; and petroleum distillates. No matter where you find them, solvent ingredients should be treated with great respect.

A GREEN WAY TO FIGHT INSIDE AIR POLLUTION

You really notice it when the air outside is polluted, especially in big cities. But do you realize the air inside buildings in can be even more polluted? In this day and age of modern, energy-efficient buildings, you might stay warmer or cooler than you used to, but such tightly sealed buildings prevent outside air from coming in and clearing the inside air of contaminants.

Some of the contaminants come from the materials used in buildings, such as particle board, insulation, synthetic carpet fibers, and carpet glue. Each of these materials give off fumes. Add this to the other pollutants present—cleaners, solvents, pesticides, office machines and more, and you have a real witches brew. The three most common pollutants in buildings today are benzene, formaldehyde, and trichloroethylene — all of which are known cancer causing agents.

"Sick Building Syndrome"

Even knowing that pollutants exist, you might not realize just how much they affect you. A new malady, known as "sick building syndrome," strikes one in five workers today. The symptoms are flu-like illnesses, nausea, headaches, skin irritations, and allergic reactions. "Sick building syndrome" may also leave you vulnerable to other illnesses. The cause of these symptoms are the contaminants people are forced to breathe everyday in their surroundings. Recent figures indicate that up to one billion dollars is lost every year in the workplace due to sick leave, lost earnings, and lost productivity.

The Cure

There are basically two ways to clean the air of indoor pollutants. The first method is to install a mechanical air purifier. These machines use activated carbon and zeolite to trap toxins like benzene and formaldehyde. Although they can be expensive, a mechanical air purifier can work well—as long as you remember to change the filter frequently.

The other method of purifying indoor air is to install plants. Yes, those same little green creatures that turned visits to Grandma's house into expeditions into the jungle. House plants thrive on toxic chemicals in their environments. Contaminants enter the leaves and soil and are transferred to the roots, which use microorganisms to break down the harmful chemicals and convert them into food.

The National Aeronautics and Space Administration (NASA) was the first organization in the U.S. to study plants as a method of removing toxic chemicals from space vehicles. Their research indicates that plants are the most effective purifiers of benzene, formaldehyde, and trichloroethylene. The nice thing is you don't have to adopt a jungle to get cleaner air. One plant is capable of cleaning 100 square feet of its environment. Consequently, the more plants you have, the better your air quality.

Any combination of household plants will work. Some plants you might consider are weeping figs, lady palms, golden pothos, corn plants, and any plants of the diffenbachia family. Plant costs range from $5-$20, and they don't need their filters changed frequently. An added benefit is plants are very eye-appealing and they can really dress up a home or business.

Some critics of the use of plants as purifiers say that with the addition of plants comes increased humidity, which leads to the growth of molds and fungi. Recent studies show this isn't the case. Although plants add humidity to a room, a definite advantage in a closed-off building, they give off a natural mold killer with the increase of moisture. They might even decrease your mold and fungi problem.

If you would like a copy of NASA's study on the effectiveness of plant purification, send a stamped, self-addressed envelope to: Plants, 10210 Bald Hill Road, Mitchellville, MD 20721.

NATURE'S CURES FOR COMMON AILMENTS

You wake up first thing in the morning and something doesn't feel quite right. Maybe you have a headache or a touch of the flu or a queasy stomach. Perhaps you didn't sleep well because of insomnia.

Whatever the problem, you've got a busy day ahead and no time to be sick—or to see a doctor. What do you do?

In today's age of busy lives and high-priced medical care, more and more people are turning to their own kitchens for the prevention and curing of minor medical problems. They do not require a doctor's prescription to use these remedies. You, too, can use items found around the house to cure yourself!

The following home remedies are for certain medical problems. Most of these cures can be found in your local supermarket or health food store. Some may already be in your refrigerator or cupboards! One thing to remember—if your medical problem persists or seems to get worse, don't hesitate to see your doctor. It might indicate that you have a serious medical problem.

Headaches

Of course, the most popular cure for a headache is an over-the-counter pain reliever like aspirin or ibuprofen. If you decide to use a pain reliever, try to take as soon after you start to feel the pain as possible. If you wait until the pain is severe, the pain relievers might not have much effect.

Another way to relieve a headache is to use ginger. Ground ginger root can prevent migraines because it blocks pain much the same way aspirin does. Also, by tying a cloth tightly around your head, you can restrict the flow of blood to your scalp. This helps to relieve the throbbing of a major migraine.

The Common, But Still Lousy, Cold

Colds have no manners. They sneak up on you when your back is turned and can make you feel lower than dirt. Fortunately, although there is no cure for the common cold, there are home remedies which can make you feel better.

One herb which can have a significant effect on a cold is garlic. Not only does garlic act like a decongestant, but it also acts like an antibiotic and can actually kill cold germs. If you are one of those people who can't stand the taste of garlic in your food, an easy way to take garlic is to swallow two or three oil-free garlic capsules three times a day until the cold is gone.

Another way to zap a cold is to take 15,000 international units (IU) each of vitamin A and beta carotene per day, along with 5,000 milligrams of vitamin C.

You can also dissolve one zinc gluconate lozenge under your tongue every three hours for the first three days, and then reduce to one lozenge every four hours for the next week. Zinc lozenges don't necessarily work for everyone, but when they do work, they can cut the average time for a cold down to four days. Zinc lozenges can also greatly reduce the dry, scratchy throat which makes colds so miserable. However, remember not to take more than the recommended amount because zinc in large doses can be toxic to the body. No one should take more than 50 milligrams of zinc per day.

The Flu

Perhaps the only thing worse than a powerful cold is a solid case of the flu. Once you get the flu, chances are you won't be able to do anything for a week. The best way to fight the flu bug is to avoid getting it. One way to protect yourself is to take 200 IUs of vitamin E every day. This is above the usual recommended daily allowance of 15 IUs, but it is still a safe amount. Vitamin E gives the immune system the boost it needs to fight infectious diseases. A good dose of vitamin C also helps the immune system fight germs. Doctors recommend taking up to 2,000 milligrams of vitamin C daily.

You can also help your body during flu season by eating healthy foods, especially foods rich in vitamin C and beta carotene like leafy green vegetables and carrots. Make sure your diet has lots of fiber and is low in fat. Getting 30 minutes of exercise three times a week can do your body a lot of good. Not only does exercise keep you in shape, but it also allows you to get rid of the stress which can put strain on your immune system. At the same time you need plenty of rest to help your body maintain its peak condition.

Another thing you can do to avoid the flu is to limit prolonged exposure to cold weather, which can weaken your immune system. It is also a very good idea to avoid sneezing, sniffling people whom you suspect have the flu—even if this means using the stairs instead of the elevator. Finally, keep the air in your home or office moist with a humidifier. Dried out nose and throat passages may make you more susceptible to viruses.

If you do all of the above and you still manage to catch the flu, you can get rid of some of the congested feeling by putting six drops of eucalyptus oil into a boiling cup of water, placing a towel over your head, and inhaling the vapors.

Wash Your Hands

Do you remember how your mother used to tell you to wash your hands after coming in from playing ball or petting the neighbor's cat, because she never knew what kinds of germs you were carrying into the house? Well, Mom was right! A little soap and water can kill infectious germs and save you a lot of money and visits to the doctor's office.

The times when it is especially important to wash your hands are:

• Before you handle or eat food

• After you use the bathroom or change a diaper

• After handling uncooked food, especially meats like chicken

• After handling money

• After blowing your nose, or sneezing or coughing into your hand

• After playing with a pet

• After taking out the garbage.

Don't be afraid to ask your health provider to wash his or her hands if you are in a clinic or hospital. Doctors and nurses are often very busy people and might forget to scrub up between patients.

Americans spend at least $20 billion every year fighting infections. When you add up the time spent and the pain suffered while curing those infections to the above figure, it is a high price to pay considering how little a bar of soap costs.

Strokes

If your family has a history of strokes, or if you, yourself, feel that you might be a candidate for a stroke at some time in the future, there is a natural way to help protect yourself. By drinking a cup or two of green tea every day, you can avoid a stroke, because green tea protects against the buildup of arterial plaque.

Breast Cancer

Breast cancer is a dreaded disease for any woman, especially if there has already been at least one case of it in the family. Medical studies show that one potential cause of breast cancer is the presence of too much of the hormone estrogen in a woman's system. You can help control your estrogen levels by eating wheat bran and any member of the cabbage family. These foods manage estrogen levels in the body. It also helps to get rid of any unnecessary body fat by trying to stay slim and within your target weight. In women, fat both produces and stores estrogen. This means that an excess of fat might also indicate an excess of estrogen in your body.

Indigestion, Heartburn and Ulcers

It happens to everybody at least once—you eat one too many helpings of Aunt Matilda's famous meatloaf, and before you know it you are nursing a good case of upset stomach. You can take an over-the-counter product to settle your stomach, but sometimes one isn't available. When all else fails, try eating a banana. Bananas can relieve indigestion. One way to fight the nausea that might come with your upset stomach is to use a little ginger.

With heartburn, the best way to avoid it is not to overindulge, especially in foods which contain lots of fat like hamburgers and French fries.You can also try drinking water with your meals to wash the stomach acids off the walls of your esophagus and back into the stomach where it belongs. Another way to avoid heartburn is to fight the temptation to snooze after meals. One of America's happiest traditions is stretching out on the sofa and watching football after Thanksgiving dinner, but this can create problems for you. By sitting upright after a big meal, gravity will help you keep the food and acids in your stomach.

If you have heartburn every day or feel a pain in your stomach, you might have an ulcer. When you suspect you have an ulcer, you should see your doctor. However, there are also things you can do around the house to make your stomach feel better. Drinking cabbage juice can help because the juice contains anti-ulcer compounds. Another way to fight an ulcer is to avoid foods which irritate it. If eating a taco with hot sauce or a hot fudge sundae bothers your stomach, don't eat it. Finally, try to cut down on the stress by exercising, letting off some steam, or just relaxing for awhile.

TIPS FOR BETTER DIETING

It happens to all of us whether we planned it or not—weight gain. The Thanksgiving turkey dinner with all the trimmings might have been the culprit which tipped the scales, or maybe the extra helpings of egg nog at Christmas. Or maybe your love of chocolate candy and apple pie finally caught up with you.

Whatever happened, there are always ways to get rid of unwanted pounds. The most popular method is going on a diet, which is an excellent way to lose pounds as long as you control the diet instead of letting the diet control you. Here are some general tips on how to control your appetite and make any diet a success.

• Give yourself time to lose weight.
Weight loss doesn't happen overnight, especially if you do it right. A good average is a pound a week. If you need to lose 50 pounds, expect it to take a year. The slower you lose weight, the more permanent your weight loss will be.

• Don't be embarrassed that you are dieting.
Instead, be proud of the fact that you are working to make yourself even better. Besides, it's hard to have fun losing weight if the whole idea makes you uncomfortable.

• Cut down on the foods you like the least.
If you never liked asparagus with cream sauce, you aren't going to miss eating that rich vegetable dish. Work to keep the foods you like the most in your diet.

• Eat your dessert first occasionally.
Think of it as giving yourself a much needed treat, while you fill yourself up so you don't overeat.

• Daydream about the life you will lead when you are thinner.
What will you do that's different? What new clothes will you try? Will you try a different hairdo?

• Change the way you do things in order to become more active.
Don't drive when you can walk. Avoid the elevator and use the stairs. Try different forms of exercise, like swimming or Nautilus, until you find something you enjoy. Introduce your body to the fun of activity.

• Eat only at the table.
With a rule like this, you avoid the diet killer of snacking in front of the TV, or carrying that roast beef sandwich to bed with you at night.

• Ban junk food from your house.
Your children might scream at this one, but why should you make it harder on yourself by watching others eat potato chips and ice cream. By introducing healthy snacks like fruit, you can introduce your children to good eating habits.

• Plan all your meals in advance, and only eat what you planned.
If you throw your meal together at the last minute, chances are it will be a high fat, high calorie dinner, or you might just settle for a box of cookies.

• Brush your teeth after every snack or meal.
When your mouth feels fresh and clean, you probably won't want to ruin that great feeling too soon by snacking on something.

• Avoid all-you-can-eat restaurants.
You can tell yourself that you will only eat healthy foods, but it is very difficult to resist creamy pastas and chocolate desserts when they are sitting out in the open where you can see them.

• Measure out medium portions of everything you eat.
If you decide to eat chips or cookies or some other treat, put a

handful in a bowl and set the bag back on the shelf. When you get to the end of the snack, it's a lot easier to say, "Enough!" if the whole bag isn't right in front of you.

• Drink a glass of water before each meal.
You need at least eight glasses of water a day anyway, and the watter will help you feel more full before you sit down to eat a regular meal.

• Chew your food slowly.
By chewing your food slowly from the beginning to the end of the meal, you slow down the speed at which you eat. It takes the brain approximately 20 minutes to get the message that the stomach is full. In 20 minutes, you can swallow a lot of food if you are eating quickly.

• Smell your food before you eat it.
This might sound really strange, but studies show that strong odors of your favorite foods may decrease your appetite. This is because the part of your brain linked to your nose also controls your body's hunger. So, the next time you sit down to food, take a deep sniff before you eat.

• Eat all meals.
No matter how tempting the thought, don't skip any meals. Skipping makes you that much hungrier the next time you eat, and you will be more inclined to gorge yourself.

• Eat complex carbohydrates.
Complex carbohydrates help your body burn calories more quickly. So, add more whole grains, pastas, peas, beans, and vegetables to each meal.

• Limit your intake of fat.
Fat has twice the calories as complex carbohydrates and it is much more likely to be stored as fat by the body. Don't completely eliminate fat, however, because your body still needs a small amount in order to stay healthy.

• Remove the skin.
Remove poultry skin before you cook the meat, because most of the fat lies just under the skin.

• Use non-stick spray.
Instead of using butter, margarine, or oil when you stir-fry or saute, give the bottom of your pan a couple of squirts of non-stick spray. This greatly reduces your fat intake and makes your food healthier.

• Don't fry.
Instead of frying your foods all the time, find other techniques which reduce the fat content of your food. Some available techniques include roasting, poaching, grilling, broiling, or micro-cooking. You can also cook food in a small amount of water or broth instead of frying.

• Keep a daily log of everything you eat.
Write down what, when, and how much you eat. Then record some short-term goals, like cutting sweets back to two items a week. Whenever you reach a goal, reward yourself with a treat that has nothing to do with food.

• Center your social events around activities instead of food.
You and your friends don't need to be parked around the sour cream chip dip in order to have a good time. Play Frisbee tag, take a walk, talk, paint, do activities which keep your mind off of food and snacking.

• Find a buddy.
For many people, it is easier to lose weight when two people try instead of one. Find someone with whom you feel comfortable and start losing weight together. You can encourage each other through the tough parts, and celebrate together as each new milestone is reached.

• Eat lean meat.
Look for meats which aren't riddled with fat and trim the visible fat from around the edges.

• Change your dressing.
Instead of drowning your salad with high fat dressings, top off your salads with cottage cheese, yogurt, or a dressing of vinegar or fruit juices mixed with seasonings.

THE DIET THAT'S GOOD FOR YOUR BODY

When you diet, it's important to remember to eat foods which are good for your entire body. Avoid getting caught in a fad diet where you eat one item forever, like grapefruit. There is nothing wrong with eating grapefruit, as long as you balance it with other nutritious foods.

By eating a variety of good foods, you not only make your body thinner, but you also help beautify your hair, skin, and nails. The secret is obtaining enough nutrients through the food you eat. Here is how to make all of your body more attractive:

• Hair.
If your hair is weak or brittle, you need to add more B-complex vitamins to your diet. Eat plenty of whole grain breads and cereals, wheat germ, green leafy vegetables, and low-fat dairy products. If you want more body and shine in your hair, add the protein found in rice, beans, lean meat, poultry, and non-oily fish to your diet.

• Skin.
To reduce problems with wrinkling, eat plenty of vitamin C found in citrus fruit, strawberries, and green peppers. Add lots of vitamin A to your diet also. Carrots, broccoli, sweet potatoes, grapes, winter squash, spinach and green peas are all important sources of vitamin A.

Wrinkled, sagging skin becomes less of a problem if you avoid yo-yo dieting. When you crash diet, losing and gaining huge amounts of weight, your skin loses its elasticity and is more susceptible to premature sagging and wrinkling. Lose weight slowly, allowing your skin to adjust to a thinner new you.

• Nails.
Nails which split and crack easily need a good diet, just like the rest of your body. If your nails are nutritionally starved, eat plenty of beans, pasta, and spinach for iron, protein, and vitamin A. Ragged cuticles need dried beans, broccoli, and green leafy vegetables— sources of folic acid vitamin C, and protein. White spots on your nails mean you need more zinc, available in nuts, or the calcium found in dairy products.

THE FAST-FOOD DIET

What if you are the kind of person who loves going to places like McDonald's or Wendy's, because the food is good and the service is fast? If the only thing which stops you from going on a diet is your love of fast food, worry no more!

You can eat at fast food restaurants three times a day and still lose up to two pounds a week. The trick is to pay attention to the caloric content of the food you order. Here are sample menus of different foods offered by 12 fast food restaurants, along with their total caloric content.

• Day 1 (1,294 calories).
BREAKFAST
Dunkin' Donuts bran muffin with raisin.......... 310
Orange juice.................................... 80
Low-fat milk.................................... 121
Total,,, 511

LUNCH
Long John Silver's Ocean Chef salad with Sea Salad dressing...240
Seafood gumbo with cod.......................... 120
Club crackers................................... 35
Black coffee, tea, or diet soda................. 0
Total... 395

DINNER
Burger King BK Broiler Chicken sandwich......... 267
Low-fat milk.................................... 121
Total... 388

• Day 2 (1,269 calories).
BREAKFAST
Arby's blueberry muffin......................... 200
Low-fat milk.................................... 121
Total... 321

LUNCH
McDonald's Filet-O-Fish sandwich................ 370

Side salad with light vinaigrette dressing........ 78
Low-fat milk.................................. 121
Total.. 558

DINNER
Wendy's 9-oz. chili............................ 220
Garden salad with reduced calorie Italian dressing......170
Black coffee, tea, or diet soda................. 0
Total.. 390

• Day 3 (1,378 calories).
BREAKFAST
McDonald's bagel............................... 240
Orange juice.................................... 80
Low-fat milk.................................... 121
Total.. 441

LUNCH
Taco Bell chicken soft taco..................... 213
Pintos 'n cheese with red sauce................. 190
Black coffee, tea, or diet soda................. 0
Total.. 403

DINNER
Kentucky Fried Chicken original recipe drumstick and breast...413
Low-fat milk.................................... 121
Total.. 534

• Day 4 (1,304 calories)
BREAKFAST
Hardee's ham biscuit........................... 320
Orange juice.................................... 80
Low-fat milk.................................... 121
Total.. 521

LUNCH
Subway small seafood and crab sandwich.......... 198
Black coffee, tea, or diet soda................. 0
Total.. 198

DINNER
Dairy Queen grilled chicken fillet sandwich..... 300

Side salad with reduced calorie French dressing.. 115
Regular cup of yogurt........................... 170
Black coffee, tea, or diet soda................ 0
Total... 585

• Day 5 (1,289 calories)
BREAKFAST
McDonald's Cheerios with low-fat milk........... 190
Fat-free apple bran muffin...................... 180
Black coffee, tea, or diet soda................ 0
Total... 370

LUNCH
Pizza Hut Thin 'n Crispy cheese pizza, 2 slices.. 398
Black coffee, tea, or diet soda................ 0
Total... 398

DINNER
Wendy's plain baked potato...................... 270
Sour cream...................................... 60
Garden salad.................................... 70
Low-fat milk.................................... 121
Total... 521

Mix and match these low-calorie meals for variety, and get plenty of exercise.

Dieting doesn't have to be painful or boring. Just remember to eat foods in moderation which taste good and are good for you. And get lots of exercise.

Don't worry if you don't feel up to trying those calorie burning aerobic dances you see on TV. A simple half hour walk or swim every day is a good way to get aerobic exercise while burning calories and building up muscle tone. Relax and enjoy your diet; make it a part of your every day existence.

SOME FINAL MEDICAL QUICKIES

Insomnia

One good way to fight insomnia is to eat some honey before bed. Honey is a sleep-inducing sedative and can have a tranquilizing effect on your tired body. A good walk, even around the block, will relax and exercise your body enough to put you to sleep. Avoid taking your work to bed. When you have papers to shuffle, chances are you won't be concentrating on sleep.

Another excellent sleep inducer involves onions. Here's what you do: A few Hours before you go to bed, slice up an onion and place it in a jar with a tight-sealed lid. Later if you find that you can't sleep, get up, find your onion jar, open it up and take a big whiff of the onion fumes that have been building up in the jar. Besides a teary face, you'll find yourself fast asleep in just five minutes! Try it! This folk remedy for sleep has been known -- and working -- for centuries!

Diarrhea

Diarrhea plays a big role in jokes about trips to foreign countries, but when you have it, it's no laughing matter. Besides over-the-counter medicines, a natural way to cure diarrhea is to take four charcoal tablets with water every hour until you are back to normal.

You can also boil one-half cup of brown rice in three cups of water and drink the water. Try drinking as many liquids as possible, but avoid milk products. Your diarrhea may be caused by a lactose intolerance, and drinking milk will just extend the time you have diarrhea. Also avoid wheat and fats.

Acne

A good way to help heal your acne is to wash your face thoroughly, especially if you use makeup. Use a mild soap twice a day and rinse the soap entirely off your face. If this doesn't work for you, try washing your face with lemon juice three times a day.

Primrose oil and chromium supplements can help if you follow the label directions. When you have a problem with acne, buy non-oil-based makeup, because oil-based makeup clogs your pores. You can also take a 100-milligram capsule of niacin with each meal.

Anemia

The best way to battle anemia is to make sure your body gets plenty of iron. Iron occurs in several kinds of food. If you think you need extra iron, especially if you are a menstruating woman, add blackstrap molasses, egg yolks, broccoli leafy greens raisins, prunes, and fish to your diet. Five hundred milligrams of raw liver extract twice a day will increase your red blood cell count. You should only take iron supplements with a doctor's permission.

Loss of Appetite

Once in awhile, we all lose our appetite because we are ill or we just don't feel like eating. If you don't feel ill and poor appetite is a problem, try eating avocados and drinking buttermilk between meals. Take 100-milligrams of vitamin B-complex daily and drink at least three cups of skim milk every day. If your loss of appetite persists, see your doctor. It might mean you have a serious illness or other medical problem which should be checked out by a professional.

Bee Stings

When you are stung by a bee, you need to remove the stinger as quickly as possible. Don't use a pair of tweezers to pull the stinger out, because that will just pump more venom from the venom sac into your system. Instead, scrape the stinger out with your fingernail. After the stinger is removed, try crushing a charcoal tablet, placing it on a cotton ball, and taping the tablet and ball over the bite area with adhesive tape to reduce the swelling. A paste of baking soda and water can also soothe the sting.

Canker Sores

Canker sores make life miserable. They hurt all the time and make your eyes water when you eat or drink the wrong kinds of foods. Drink red raspberry tea or eat salads with onions and garlic if you have a pesky canker sore. Put a wet black tea bag over the sore. Tea cleans out the wound and can kill the pain. Try to avoid eating certain foods like sugar, processed foods, citrus fruits, coffee, fish, and mouthwashes.

Poison Ivy

You go on a nature walk through the woods with your family. The object is to collect as many different leaves as possible. Little Jimmy comes to you with a handful of pretty specimens. You suddenly realize to your horror Little Jimmy has innocently picked— POISON IVY! What on earth are you going to do?

The most important thing you can do is make sure Jimmy washes his hand with soap and water as soon after exposure as possible. If he still ends up with poison ivy you can apply compresses soaked in a mixture of one pint Burrow's solution and 15 pints of cool water to relieve the itching. By taking 3,000-milligrams of vitamin C every day, you can prevent infection and the spreading of the rash. You might also consider becoming intimately acquainted with a bottle of calamine lotion.

MEDICAL TOPICS SECTION ENDS HERE

Mastering Super Reading

Have you ever noticed how some people seem to effortlessly grasp the meaning of everything they read? What is more, they remember all the right stuff and can answer the toughest questions on a test or in a discussion or meeting. How did they do that?

Chances are, these "super readers" learned the right questions to ask while reading. In fact, they learned how to read. Proper reading skills do not appear overnight; they require frequent use before you can completely master them. But the interesting thing about building reading skills is that it is something you will use the rest of your life, and you can learn all the secrets of good reading in nine easy steps. Whether you are a college student studying for a test, a parent trying to help your teenage daughter through high school, or a factory employee who has a lunch break to read and remember the latest manual, you will find that good reading skills are an invaluable part of your life.

GET INVOLVED

The most important thing you need to remember about good reading is to get involved with the book. If you passively read your book without putting some brainpower into what you are doing, you are going to fail. You may as well put the book under your pillow at night and hope the right answers seep into your brain while you sleep. Remember—every time you read a book, you talk to the author. In order to get the most out of your reading, you need to question the author, search for answers, and argue, if necessary. The following are nine questions you can use to improve your reading skills and find out what the author is talking about. Ask yourself:

Why am I reading this?

You can save a lot of time by deciding whether you need specific facts or more general ideas before you begin reading. If you want specific facts, you can probably skim through the whole book quickly or even skip parts, thereby saving loads of time. There is no cardinal law that says you have to read every word in a book.

Do I already know about this topic?

Before you open a book, take some time to make a few notes about what you already know about the book's topic, what you can guess, and what you might like to learn. This prepares you for asking relevant questions as you begin reading. It also allows you to think for yourself. You are in a better position to question the author's ideas and won't be so easily swayed by them.

After making your notes, skim the entire book. Pay special attention to the introduction, table of contents, chapter summaries, index, and the author's biography. These parts of the book don't have to be boring. They save huge amounts of reading time by informing you on exactly what the book is about.

What's the big idea?

As you begin reading, jot down the author's main points. With the main points in front of you, it won't be as easy to get lost in the book's small details. Make a game of your search. Pretend the author has hidden a treasure and it is up to you to find all the clues which will lead you to the pot at the end of the rainbow.

What will the author say next?

Try to anticipate where the author is going with his or her information. Sometimes you might be wrong, but even with new material you can probably make a reasonable guess.

What are the expert questions?

Often books, especially text books, have questions built into them. For example, history books often answer questions like "When did it happen?," "What were the causes?," 'What were the results?," Finding the expert questions usually leads you to the main or important points.

What are my questions?

As you read, questions will probably develop in your mind about what you are reading. Let your curiosity run wild by asking— and then trying to answer—your questions. Sometimes your speculations will be exactly right, sometimes completely wrong. It doesn't matter as long as you work with the author to find the answers. You might even decide to read more books on the subject to explore unanswered questions.

What information should I use?

The answer to this question depends on why you read the book in the first place. Don't bother taking notes on material you never planned on using. If you were looking for specific facts, stick with those facts. In general, 80 percent of the information will be found in about 20 percent of the book.

How do I summarize my information?

In your own words, briefly summarize what you have learned from the book. Keep your summary as brief—and as accurate—as possible, because the shorter it is, the easier it will be to remember. If you copy key points out of the book without using your own words, you probably didn't understand what the author was talking about.

How do I organize my information?

Try rearranging the material into a form that makes sense. The organization might include diagrams, sketches, bits of sentences, whatever helps you to remember. Work to fit all of the information onto one page, and then study that page until you can reproduce it from memory. Now you are ready to make use of what you learned from the book.

This may sound like a great deal of work, but a little practice will make these steps second nature.. It may surprise you to see just how much material you remember using this system. Best of all, you take charge of life as the prospect of learning new information becomes less and less frightening.

WAYS TO DEAL WITH YOUR CREDIT

If you are like many people in the United States today, you probably own at least one credit card on which you've made purchases, along with long term loans for cars, houses, boats, or post-secondary education. And like many Americans, you may find it difficult sometimes to make all the payments on what you owe.

The secret to a healthy financial life is to know how to handle credit, keep track of what you spend, and maintain a good credit history. Here are a few tips on how to turn your personal finances around:

CREDIT CARDS

These days, you may think it's difficult to operate without at least one credit card. "Plastic money" makes it easy to make purchases when you don't have your checkbook or spare cash on hand. Places like hotels, car rental agencies, and ticket outlets require credit cards before you can make reservations. Some businesses even require a card as identification before they will accept your check.

But if you aren't watching your funds carefully, you can easily end up deeply in debt. Just because a major credit card company extends $5,000 credit to you, it doesn't mean you are worth that extra $5,000. The trick is to spend within your budget. Credit cards aren't necessarily evil devices—you just have to know how to handle them wisely. Here are some ideas on managing your cards:

• Remember that for every purchase you make with a credit card, you stand a good chance of being charged a high rate of interest for any money used in your purchase. For example, you buy a new lawn mower with your credit card for $1,000. Your card has a typical annual interest amount of 18.5 percent, and it takes you a whole year to pay off the mower. Your lawn mower ends up costing you about $1,185 by the time you finish paying for it. Since this is not the only purchase you make in a year, the interest really begins to add up.

If you need to buy an item right away, it's okay to use your card, but work to get the item paid off before the end of the month. Most cards won't charge you interest that way.

In a sense, you can earn over 18 percent on your money by paying off your card debts early. If you use $100 to pay off a credit card debt charging you 18.5 percent interest, you would save $18.48 in after-tax-dollars on your finance charges in the course of a year. That's a return of 18.48 percent on your money!

• Write a check for an item, instead of yanking out the plastic cash for each purchase. Credit cards are easy to use, and some card companies even advertise that they want you to use cards on all purchases, even groceries. They say it's much easier to keep track of what you buy because at the end of the month you get one printout of all purchases. The problem is that convenience really costs. If you charge $400 worth of groceries each month on an 18.5 percent card, those groceries end up costing $474—almost another whole week's worth of food!

• For major purchases, like lawn mowers, furniture, or appliances, see if there are other ways to finance them at lower interest rates than your card provides. Go to a bank and see if you can borrow at 8-12 percent interest for a period of time. Or check the appliance and furniture stores. Many offer their customers loans at 10-12 percent, pending credit approval. Anything is better than paying 18.5 percent on all purchases.

• Keep your card only for emergencies. This is especially true if you travel a lot and your vehicle breaks down. It is great to have a $3,000 or $5,000 cushion in order to have repairs done so you can get going again. However, as mentioned before, try to get those charged repairs paid for as soon as possible.

If having your card in your billfold is too much of a temptation, freeze it in a bag half-filled with water. Freezing it won't hurt the magnetic strip, but it will give you enough time while the card thaws to decide if a purchase really is an emergency.

• Shop around for low interest credit cards.
The lower the interest on your credit cards, the better off you are at the end of the fiscal year. The chart below shows how a 11.5 percent fixed-rate card with a $25 annual fee stacks up against other annual fees. The amounts in the chart show how much more you save with the 11.5 percent card.
Average Annual

	16%	17%	17.95%	19%	19.8%
Balance					
$1,000	$45	$55	$64.5	$75	$83
$2,000	$90	$110	$129	$150	$166
$3,000	$135	$165	$193.5	$225	$249
$5,000	$225	$275	$322.5	$375	$415

· **Beware low, low credit offers!**

At some time or other, you will probably get an invitation in the mail to shift your credit card account to a new card which offers you an incredible six percent interest rate.

Whatever you do, read the fine print and make sure of what you are getting into before you transfer your account. Often, the fine print will reveal that the interest rate is good only for the next six months, or that it only applies to the balance of what you transfer over.

Two credit card companies who recently promoted very low interest rates are Citibank and Nations Bank. Citibank allowed other cardholders to transfer their balances to Citibank cards to take advantage of 9.9 percent interest. However, after March 1994 the interest jumped to around 15 percent.

In the case of Nations Bank, the company offered six percent interest in a special mail offer. After February 1994, interest rates for people who responded to the offer jumped to 9.9 percent plus the prime rate. The cardholders who transferred their accounts found themselves paying more than 15 percent!

If an offer sounds too good to be true, read the fine print to see if there is a catch.

CREDIT REPAIR ORGANIZATIONS (CROS)

Your credit history is extremely important, especially if you ever plan on securing a loan, a lease on an apartment, or even to cash a check sometimes. A credit history includes all information about any loans you've made, including credit cards, student loans, and car payments, and the history you have of paying back your loans on time.

If you have a good payback reputation, the sky can be the limit. But if your reputation is less than sterling, chances are you will have a lot of trouble getting money when you need it. Be very careful, however, calling in a credit repair organization to fix your credit history. Although some are legitimate, many rip-off their customers by promising more than they can deliver.

In theory, CROs are set up to provide customers with a chance to remove any bad loans from their credit history. They sometimes charge hundreds of dollars for this service. The reality of CROs is that they cannot, by law, remove any correct, unfavorable item from your credit report. Some, however, create the illusion of doing this by using the complicated credit reporting system to their own advantage.

With a typical bad CRO, the organization might flood credit bureaus with disputes regarding unfavorable but accurate items in a customer's file. Because of a 30-day limit in which a credit bureau can conduct its investigation, the disputed item is pulled temporarily from the record until it can be further investigated. The CRO can then report back to its customer that the unfavorable item is officially removed from the credit history. What the CRO doesn't mention is that the item returns to the file after 30 days, and the customer is no better off than before.

Only time can heal a bad credit report. However, if you want to hire a CRO to handle a credit history investigation, check its reputation first with your state's regulatory agencies.

• The do-it-yourself credit investigation.
You can save a lot of money—and probably more than a few headaches—by checking your credit history yourself. There is nothing a CRO does that you cannot do for yourself. There are several ways you can monitor your credit history and correct any inaccurate errors yourself:

√ Review your credit history on a regular basis, at least once a year or several months before you plan to make a major purchase. You can get a copy of your credit report for $8-10 from one of the three main credit agencies. Write to:
* Equifax, Box 740241, Atlanta, GA 30374, (800-685-1111).
* Trans Union, Box 7000, North Olmsted, OH 44070, (313-689-3888). The report costs $8 per copy, unless you were denied credit within the last 60 days, whereby you get a free copy.
* TRW; National Consumer Relations Center; 12606 Greenville Ave., Box 749029; Dallas, TX 75374-9029, (214-235-1200). Trw offers one free credit report annually. If you want to take advantage of this offer, write to: TRW, Box 2350, Chatsworth, CA 91313-2350.

It is a good idea to obtain a copy from all three companies to make sure they all list the same items.

√ If you find an error, fill out the dispute form which comes with your credit report and return it to the credit bureau. The credit bureau will contact the company with whom you have a disagreement, and will either verify the standing record or change the entry within 30 days.

√ If you feel you aren't getting anywhere with the credit bureau because they are ignoring you or mishandling your report, you can complain to the FTC at: Federal Trade Commission, Correspondence Dept./Room 692, Washington, D.C. 20580.

Your financial life doesn't have to be a complete mystery to you. By keeping track of where your money goes, finding ways to save money, and maintaining an accurate credit report, you can have a good handle on what happens to your finances, and no nasty surprises will await you in the mailbox or local bank.

SAFETY PRECAUTIONS AGAINST CRIME

In today's world, where the news media seem to cover more and more thefts, rapes, and murders, the average American citizen doesn't appear to be safe anymore. If you fear being just another victim, you are not alone—and you don't have to simply put up with your fears. There are many things you can do to insure that you don't become just another crime statistic. Some of the following suggestions may seem elementary and simplistic, but they may be all that keep you from being a victim of crime.

If you want to avoid being a victim, you can:

• Avoid using cash machines. Instead, plan ahead and use the main part of the bank for your transactions. More and more people are experiencing robberies, kidnappings, and even murders after a criminal nails them at an automatic cash machine. Even with the surveillance cameras set up by banks, there is no guarantee the bad guys won't get you.

• Don't give people an opportunity to see just how much cash you have. The best way to avoid this is to pull enough cash out of your money roll to pay for your next purchase and put it in one pocket—and then put the main roll someplace else.

• Don't wear expensive jewelry. You might be very proud of that brand-new diamond and emerald cocktail ring your husband gave you as an anniversary present, but it can mark you as a victim. If you aren't sure of the area you're in, take the rings off or drop the necklaces inside your blouse. Or better yet, leave them at home.

• When walking, stay away from buildings, parked cars, trees, and shrubs where muggers can hide. Also, avoid walking or jogging in isolated areas and during hours when no one is usually around, like Central Park at 3 a.m.

• Keep your keys in your hand when walking to and from your vehicle. Then you will be ready for a quick exit, if necessary.

• If someone acts suspicious, walk in the opposite direction, duck into a store or cafe, or cross the street.

• Drive with your windows rolled up and your doors locked, and don't pick up strangers. Even when someone flags you down for help, don't stop. It could be a set-up for a car-jacking. Drive to the nearest phone, instead, and notify the police of an emergency.

• Use busy, well-lighted streets at night and stay out of dark, isolated neighborhoods. This especially applies when you are a stranger to the area.

• If someone bumps your car, especially after dark, don't stop. Drive to the nearest police station or police car instead. If the bump was purely an accident, you can straighten it out with a policeman present. However, car bumping is a favorite gimmick for car-jackers and thieves.

You can also do many things to secure your home. Most home burglaries are committed by amateur and semi-professional burglars who find an easy entrance to the house. By making a few simple, unobtrusive changes in the way your home presents itself, you can cut your chances of burglary by as much as 95 percent.

Here's how:

• Arrange your outdoor lighting so that it is directed outward and crosswise, instead of leaving parts of your yard in shadow. A number of yard, porch, and floodlights left on all night allows you to see someone approaching the house, while the glare prevents a burglar from seeing you observing him.

• Put up a security fence around your house. This is particularly effective in daylight when a significant number of residential burglaries occur. The fence should be at least five feet high with points on top and as few horizontal pieces as possible. A nice wrought iron fence serves the purpose very well and can add a lot to the appearance of your property.

• Install a minimum of one one-inch deadbolt to each solid wood or metal door. Wherever doors or adjacent panels are made partly from glass, install double cylinder locks which need keys both inside and out. All of your double cylinder locks can be adjusted to accept the same key. If you have to, replace your vulnerable windows with break-resistant materials, like lexan.

• Replace your standard sash-mounted window locks with modern security devices, or with strong pins or nails which run through solid wood or metal to prevent window movement.

• Remember your garage during your burglar-proofing, especially if it is attached to the house. Put a good lock on the walk-through door and consider using hinged overhead garage doors on tracks, which are more resistant to forced entry.

• Make it look as if someone is always in the house. When you go out on errands, leave the radio or TV on loud enough for someone to hear it outside. Also, light timers can turn different lights on at specific times, making your house appear lived-in, even when you are on vacation.

• Check all strangers' credentials. Everyone in the house, even the children, should know to ask all sales people and repair people for their credentials before allowing them indoors. If a stranger refuses to identify himself, don't let him in the house. Also, beware of anyone who insists on coming inside to make an emergency phone call. If it really is an emergency, you can make the call for him.

• If you feel threatened in any way, don't hesitate to scream or call the police.

The important thing is to think safety. If an incident doesn't feel right, chances are it means trouble. This doesn't mean you have to barricade yourself in your house with an arsenal—just take a few precautions. For people who don't like being alone, consider getting a dog. Even the friendliest breeds, like golden retrievers and beagles, can make great companions and good watch dogs.

HOW SAFE ARE YOUR BANK ACCOUNTS

If you haven't checked your bank accounts lately because you think the Federal Deposit Insurance Corporation (FDIC) will protect everything you have, you'd better take a second look.

The FDIC still covers accounts up to $100,000 in the banks which it protects. However, depending on how your accounts are set up, the corporation might not be covering all the money you've put into banks. Also, although the FDIC covers most banks, it does not protect some privately owned banks. If your bank is protected, you will see a FDIC sign on the door of the bank or next to the tellers.

Here are some common misconceptions about FDIC protection:

• All individual accounts are covered separately by the FDIC.
This depends on the total amount of your individual accounts. The FDIC does cover individual accounts up to $100,000, but most people don't realize that an individual account is determined by adding up each account held under a common name or Social Security number.

For example, if you have a $70,000 savings account and a $50,000 certificate of deposit (CD) in your name at the same bank, $20,000 of your funds are not protected by the FDIC. If you have set up an account under the Uniform Gifts to Minors Act, the account is in the child's name, even though the parent controls it.

• All bank deposits are covered by the FDIC.
False. Mutual funds and other investments made through a bank are not covered by the FDIC.

• Joint accounts are fully protected by the FDIC.
Once again, this depends on the total amount of your joint account. Any combination of accounts held by the same people is protected up to $100,000, regardless of the Social Security numbers which appear on the accounts. For example, if you and your spouse control two joint accounts of $100,000 each, $100,000 of your $200,000 worth of accounts is not covered by the FDIC. One way around this restriction is to have a combination of joint and individual accounts.

• Accounts opened at different branches of the same bank are each protected by the FDIC.
False. The only way you can get FDIC coverage for all of your accounts is by dividing your funds among several separate banks.

• All trust accounts are treated separately by the FDIC.
True—as long as the trust account is opened for members of your immediate family, such as your spouse, child (including step and adopted children), or grandchildren. You can still enjoy FDIC coverage on individual and joint accounts if you set up a trust for immediate family members. If you open a trust for your father or mother, however, the money will still be considered part of your account.

• IRAs and Keoghs are fully protected by the FDIC.
As of December 19, 1993, individual retirement accounts (IRAs) and Keoghs are lumped together when establishing coverage limits. For example, if you have $100,000 in IRAs and $50,000 in Keoghs in the same bank, $50,000 of your money is left unprotected by the FDIC.

The best way to take care of your money is to divide your funds among several safe banks in your area, keeping no more than $100,000 in any one establishment. For a list of the safest banks in your state, send $5 to Veribane, P.O. Box 461, Wakefield, MA 01880.

By arranging your finances wisely, you can make sure your money is there for you when you need it. In this day and age of failed banks and savings and loans, you can no longer afford to leave all your funds tied up in the same place. For more information on FDIC insurance, call the FDIC at 800-934-3342.

STEPS TO FINDING A GOOD FINANCIAL PLANNER

With the ever increasing growth of potential investments on today's market, you might find it difficult to know exactly where to invest your money. When this becomes a problem for you, it is a good idea to seek out the advice of a financial planner.

The goal of a good financial planner is to find investments which are tailor-made to your personal needs, whether you need help getting started in investments, managing your assets, or avoiding taxes. But how can you tell the good planners from the bad?

Unfortunately, a good financial planner can be hard to find. In a business where more than 200,000 people call themselves financial planners, only about 40,000 have completed any course work. Also, financial planning does not receive much governmental scrutiny, and the Securities and Exchange Commission (SEC) has not increased its numbers of inspectors to oversee planners.

Basically, anyone can hang up a sign and call himself a financial planner. This translates into at least $300 million in customer losses every year. When you began searching for a financial planner, there are some things to look for which will help you decide whether or not the planner you contract with is qualified.

CERTIFIED FINANCIAL PLANNERS (CFP)

The first item to look for is whether the planner is certified. Look for "CFP" somewhere within the name of the business. This indicates that the planner has taken the required 30 seminar hours over each two year period. The certified financial planner also has a certain amount of experience in the field. Like a lawyer or any other professional, a CFP takes a comprehensive two-day examination.

The CFPs are policed by the licensing body that certified them, which makes sure the public isn't misled. Most CFPs are also registered with the SEC and state regulatory agencies.

TYPES OF FINANCIAL PLANNERS

An investor today can choose between three kinds of financial planners—"fee only" planners, hybrid planners, or "commission only" planners.

· Fee only planners

These planners charge either an annual fee or an hourly rate, which starts at about $100 and might increase to over $250. Fee only planners are your best bet, because they tend to be the most trustworthy. With you paying their rates up front, there is less of a likelihood of them taking cuts from insurance companies, mutual fund families or banks for steering you to their products.

· Hybrid planners

Hybrids charge a flat fee and might also take a commission for any insurance or investments purchased through them.

· Commission only planners

You have to be careful with this group, because they have a great interest in selling you particular investments for commissions. They might not have your best interests in mind.

HOW TO FIND A PLANNER

Before you begin searching for a planner, you need to decide where you need help. Are you looking for advice on starting an investment portfolio, or maintaining one, or perhaps avoiding taxes? Whichever kind of advice you need, you should gear any questions you might have for a potential planner toward answering your needs.

Next, compile a list of planners in your area, and check with state regulatory agencies on whether any of them have faced disciplinary actions. If you need help finding a reputable planner, contact one of the following addresses:

Institute of Certified Financial Planners (ICFP); 600 E. Eastman Ave., Suite 301; Denver, CO 80231-4397, (800-322-4237 for information services, or 800-282-7526). ICFP provides you with a list of CFPs in your area. There are more than 7,000 CFPs nationwide working full-time at financial planning.

National Association of Personal Financial Advisors (NAPFA); 1130 Lake Cook Road, Suite 105; Buffalo Grove, IL, (708-537-7722 or 800-366-2732). NAPFA will give you a list of full-time fee only planners in your area. There are only about 300 full-time fee only planners in the U.S.

Make a list of at least three financial planners you would like to contact. Call each planner on your list and ask them four basic questions:

• What is your fee structure?
Good financial planners are more than happy to disclose their fee structures. Make sure you get a written estimate of what your potential needs will cost before you decide on a particular planner.

• Do you have a working network with other planners?
Because it is very unlikely for one planner to know everything about all forms of investments, you would be wise to make sure your planner is in contact with other planners in order to draw on their expertise.

• What is your investment strategy?
If you have to, ask the planner how he or she would invest a hypothetical sum of money on the current market. If you turn over some of your portfolio for the planner to manage, demand returns at least a few points above risk free investments like Treasury bills.

• Who are your references?
Ask the planner to supply several references—at least enough to track the planner's performance throughout both a bull and a bear market. The list will probably be biased, but at least you might learn something about how the planner treats his customers.

It is also a great idea to visit each potential financial planner in his or her office for a face-to-face interview. And don't be buffaloed by what they say. If you feel uncomfortable with a planner, just say no. It's your money and you should decide who handles it.

If you do have trouble with a certified financial investor and you feel that he or she didn't handle your money correctly, contact the CFP licensing body and register a complaint. Their address is:

International Board of Standards and practices for certified Financial Planners (IBCFP); 1660 Lincoln Street, Suite 3050; Denver, CO 80264, (303-830-7543).

MUTUAL FUND PLANNERS

You should also be aware that several mutual fund families offer free financial advice. A particular example of this is Fidelity Investments. The minimum deposit to open a non-retirement account at Fidelity is $200,000, or $100,000 for an Individual Retirement Account.

Fidelity planners discuss and manage your portfolio on a one-to-one basis. The company has over 200 funds which they can tailor to your individual needs. For more information, contact Fidelity Portfolio Advisory Services at 800-544-3455.

SAVE MONEY BY BUYING FROM UNCLE SAM

How would you like to buy cars, cellular phones, clothing, perfume, or jewelry at rock bottom prices? If you are at all interested, check out a government auction. The U.S. Government often finds itself in possession of a lot of unnecessary material, which it has to get rid of. The property is either government surplus or items seized by federal agencies.

With a bit of luck and some knowledge about how government auctions run, you can walk away with bargains like a Porsche for under $14,000, a Lincoln Continental for under $1,000, or a $100,000 airplane for as little as $15,000. You simply need to know where and how to shop for these fantastically reduced rates.

GOVERNMENT SURPLUS

Like any other business, the federal government has to get rid of excess material at the end of every year in order to make room for new stuff. The government spends billions of dollars each year on equipment and supplies. Anything left over is labeled "surplus" and sold at government auction.

Some of the material auctioned off includes cars and trucks, hardware, furniture, processors, printers, and cash registers. For example, if you are looking for a good used car, the government sells a great many three- to four-year-old domestic model four-door sedans with odometer readings of between 30,000 and 70,000 miles for as little as $3,000.

The Department of Defense (616-961-7331) and the General Services Administration (800-GSA-1313) alone dispose of over $120 million in surplus every year. Call these departments for further information.

SEIZURES AND IMPOUNDMENTS

We have all heard of the Drug Enforcement Agency (DEA) and the Federal Bureau of Investigation (FBI) seizing property belonging to some big drug lord in Florida. However, these belongings are not the only material which appears at government impoundment auctions. U.S. Customs and the Internal Revenue Service (IRS) are also big sources for seized items.

U.S. Customs often takes items away from people reentering this country who cannot or will not pay duties on belongings bought in a foreign country. Everything from jewelry, watches, and perfumes to electronics, clothing and liquor appear at U.S. Customs auctions. The company EG&G Dynatrend conducts Customs Service auctions in many major cities. For further information, write to: EG&G Dynatrend; U.S. Customs Service Support Division; 2300 Clarendon Blvd., Suite 705; Arlington, VA 22201 and ask for their booklet, "Public Auctions." Or call the Public Auction Line at 703-351-7887.

The IRS seizes property and forces sales in order to collect money for back taxes. Call 800-829-1040 to get on the IRS auction mailing list.

Property seized by the FBI or the DEA is auctioned off by the U.S. Marshals Service, a branch of the Justice Department. The FBI and DEA often end up with property like motorcycles, cameras, personal computers, and TV sets. For more information on U.S. Marshals Service sales, check the classified ads of your local newspapers, or look in the Wednesday copy of USA Today.

GOVERNMENT AUCTION PROCEDURES

Procedures can be different from auction to auction, but in general you register at the site before a sale. By registering, you receive a sales catalog and bidder number. Many government auctions are open bid, with an auctioneer calling out prices. Here are a few tips which will allow you to get the most out of a government auction:

• Always inspect the merchandise on which you plan to bid. Almost everything from vehicles to video equipment is sold "as is" and without any warranty or guarantees. Sometimes the viewing time is scheduled for a different day than the sale date, so you might have to plan two trips.

• Government auction property is sold either individually or by lot. Make sure you are buying the amount you want. You might think you are bidding on one 10-foot plastic pipe and discover you bought 100.

• Find out payment terms before you get to the auction. While some sales accept personal checks and credit cards, many will take only cash or cashier's checks.

Government auctions can be great places to find bargains on equipment, especially if you are trying to outfit a new business. Like any other sale, however, know what you are getting before you buy it.

HOW TO OUTSMART YOUR SUPERMARKET

Have you ever strolled into a supermarket planning on buying a few essentials, like bread or milk, and walked out with a lot more food than you bargained for? It happens all the time. As you walk past the fresh produce, you notice the Bing cherries are on sale, so you grab a pound or two. Aisle number two is crowded, so you take a short cut to the back where the milk is by making a tour through the pet supply aisle. Unloaded boxes of detergent temporarily block the aisle, so while you wait, you notice the most adorable new dog toy that Fido simply must have! Finally, the way is clear and you make it back to the milk.

Your odyssey isn't over, however, because you still have to survive the fresh baked goods and deli section. After choosing two kinds of bread, a pound of deli-sliced roast beef, and a dozen cream-filled Bismarcks, you are ready to check out. As you pass the frozen foods, a lady gives you a sample of a new variety of pizza that tastes so good, you buy one for lunch. At the check-out stand, you notice a glaring headline—I GAVE BIRTH TO A TWO HEADED MARTIAN AND A PARTRIDGE IN A PEAR TREE. That's a provocative idea, so you grab the magazine, pay for everything, and rush out the door before something else captures your attention—and your pocket book. The trip to the supermarket which should have cost about $5 ended up taking a nice $23.35 out of your checking account. How on earth did that happen?

The key is supermarkets are set up expressly to get as much spare change as possible out of you. Every inch of the store is planned, from the fresh fruit at the entrance to the boxes left casually in the middle of the floor. Let's take a tour of the typical supermarket and see just exactly how and why the store is laid out the way it is.

• As you enter the store, the first thing you fall over is a wall of seasonal "bargains." In the summer, this wall includes charcoal and charcoal fluid, soda, watermelons, and sweet corn. At Christmas, you can probably buy holiday candy and cookies, and nuts in the shell. The store management built that wall to slow you down. Even if you don't buy any seasonal product, you've paused just long enough to notice. . . .

• The produce department—many supermarkets stake their reputation on how fresh their fruit looks. If the fruit looks high quality, a typical shopper assumes everything else in the store is the best quality, too. Fruit is an impulse buy for many people, so if you walk away with even one banana you didn't originally intend to get, the produce department has done its job.

• As you walk through the produce, you might notice that some items, like bottled salad dressing, is stored smack-dab between the lettuce and the tomatoes. If you didn't see the three together and thought how good they would taste, would you really have bought lettuce, tomatoes, and the expensive variety of salad dressing?

• You might also notice a nice display of fresh flowers and green plants near the produce area. Plants are also a great item for impulse buyers, and they slow you down even further as you stop to admire the pretty floral displays.

• You turn the corner and there are the island-shaped refrigerator cases. Unlike the old-fashioned cases which rested against the wall, island-shaped cases allow shoppers to buy from all sides. Probably you make a complete tour of the case just to see what's inside, and your shopping slows down once again.

• You finally get to the dairy section, which is located usually in back at the farthest possible corner from the entrance. The management figures everyone buys eggs or milk each trip. By making you walk all the way to the back every time, you have to travel through all the displays set up to attract your attention—and your money.

• As you pass the ends of the aisles, you notice a number of sale items are displayed there. What you might not notice is there are also several products which are not on sale. If you aren't paying attention, you might mistake one for the other.

• The bakery and deli is always located at the front of the store so the lovely smells of rolls, baked bread, and roasted chicken attract your attention the second you walk into the store. Who can resist snapping up a pastry or two on the way out?

• As a last minute attempt to get your money, the management puts high-margin items, like candy, batteries, magazines, and doodads, where you can stare at them as you wait in the check-out line. Anyone who has ever been grocery shopping with small children knows the second they see the candy, they make a grab for it. Since there are several seconds while waiting in line, it takes a strong parent not to silence their children's wails by buying candy bars for the whole family.

OTHER STORE TACTICS:

· In-store Marketing.
One tactic stores began using a few years ago is a device called in-store marketing. Manufacturers rent shelf space from supermarkets to prominently display their products. Usually, this means the big brand names are placed at eye level, where they are easy to reach, and brands which do not rent space land on the top or bottom shelves, a more inconvenient location.

For example, you might see cans of Dole pineapple on shelf three on a four shelf tier, while a lesser known brand of pineapple ends up on the bottom shelf. Staples like salt, sugar, and flour are always placed on the bottom shelf, because people need them anyway and will be willing to bend over to get them.

In-store marketing sometimes prevents smaller companies from competing for space, because they can't afford to pay the prices. And the extra money manufacturers pay for shelf space and in-store promotions is possibly passed on to consumers.

· Coupons

Another trick supermarkets and product companies use is they distribute coupons. Coupons can be a terrific thing and can help you save a great deal of money over time. However, if coupons make you buy something you wouldn't ordinarily get because you think you are receiving a good bargain, you aren't saving money.

Take snack crackers, for example. You normally don't buy snack crackers, but suddenly you find a $.50 coupon in a paper for a new snack cracker shaped like a firecracker. You buy the item for $1.75. Although you saved $.50 on the purchase, you spent $1.25 more than you originally planned.

Supermarkets also use a concept known as "loss leaders" to get more people into the store. They markdown an item or distribute a store coupon for something that normally isn't cheap, like hamburger for $.98 a pound. The idea is as people enter the store to take advantage of the loss leader, they also buy other items which attract them, like hamburger buns, mustard, and a bouquet of freshly cut flowers.

· Layout and design

Besides the layout tips related above, another tactic used by supermarkets to slow down your shopping trip is the ever present box-in-the-aisle. Occasionally, grocers go too far with this plan. They put so much stuff in the aisles to slow down customers that the place resembles a maze or obstacle course, and shoppers end up frustrated.

Sometimes stores go a long way to project an image of low prices and cost cutting. A few supermarket chains house their stores in warehouse-like buildings with pipes showing in the roof and products displayed on plain gray metal shelves. It's a good idea to compare prices, even in stores like this, because sometimes they don't live up to their image.

· Product tie-ins

Supermarket management notices that when dip goes on sale, the amount of potato chips bought also goes up. This is known as a product tie-in. Sometimes it works in your favor, especially if you buy chips every week anyway. However, sometimes the prices of items like hamburgers or hot dogs are greatly reduced, and the supermarkets make up the difference by selling you charcoal, ketchup, and buns at normal prices.

· Automated checkout systems

If you have ever wondered whether the scanner at the checkout is always accurate, the answer is no. With so many items going on sale every week, sometimes store employees don't get all of sale items tagged on the shelves—or marked down in the computer.

Not too long ago, I bought some bread, soda, a pizza, and some apples at a local supermarket. The soda and pizza were both on sale. By watching the amounts as the bar codes were scanned, I noticed the pizza and soda had the regular price listed. After pointing out the discrepancy to the store employee, I saved about $4 on my grocery bill.

The best ways to make sure you get accurate prices are to write the sale prices down on your shopping list, or check the register tape against the sales flyer when you get home. If you find a discrepancy, supermarkets are more than willing to refund the difference.

Supermarkets are not the only ones who work hard to sell you on the image of their stores—manufacturers also work hard on image when they package their products.

Often, manufacturers use packaging to make the buyer think that what's inside is much better than the competitors' brands. Wheaties, for example, uses "the Breakfast of Champions" as its slogan. To further convey this image, the box is a bright, vibrant orange, and often sports heroes are pictured on the front of the box. This might make a consumer believe if he eats Wheaties, he, too, can knock over a 40-foot tall oak with a single stroke.

Manufacturers even try to convince you there are differences within their own product lines. The supermarket A&P carries its traditional Eight O'Clock coffee beans for $3.25. At the same time, their specialty "Royale" coffee beans cost $4.99. Although the "Royale" coffee is advertised as a supremely special variety with its own gold bag, the difference between the two varieties of coffee was one of size, not quality. The "Royale" coffee beans are somewhat larger than the Eight O'Clock beans.

• Manufacturers occasionally try for the homemade look with their packaging. Classico pasta sauce comes in a mason jar, as if your grandmother processed and canned it just last week. B&M baked beans are packaged in a brown glass crock reminiscent of the old crocks once used by Boston baked bean makers—and your great-grandmother. Even supermarkets get in on packaging by selling unsliced bread baked in their own kitchens. It may not exactly taste homemade, but it certainly looks the part.

• Consumer convenience can be a major determiner of packaging. Once upon a time, you bought chicken one way—whole and in a plain plastic bag. Now, most chickens are cut up and sorted before you even see them for sale. You can buy legs, thighs or breasts, and chickens which are de-boned, de-fatted, and de-skinned. It's a tremendous convenience for the shopper, who no longer has to cut up his own chicken or wonder what to do with certain parts, like necks and backs. However, you pay more for your chicken because of the convenience.

Another consumer convenience are the already shredded vegetables you can find in the produce section. It is very nice not to have to peel and shred your own carrots or chop your cabbage, but you end up with perhaps a 400 percent markup for the convenience.

What can a shopper do to avoid these supermarket pitfalls? Here are some suggestions:

• Clip coupons only for products you usually buy anyway.

• Stick to your shopping list. If you see something you would like to buy on impulse, like a plant, write it down for next week's list. Maybe it won't seem so important then. Some supermarkets run unadvertised sales as added incentives for shoppers who are already in the store. When you see a good bargain, it is okay to stray somewhat from your shopping list.

• Comparison shop among different sales flyers and supermarkets, and keep track of prices.

• If you can't find the price for an item listed anywhere on the shelf, don't be afraid to ask an employee. Spotty price lists are one main complaint made by supermarket shoppers. You don't have to settle for buying a product you don't even know the price of.

• Stock up on items when they are on sale. This is especially true with high-priced items like peanut butter and coffee. Buying in bulk can save you a lot of money.

• Pick up hot specials on items you use regularly. Many supermarket chains regularly reduce the prices of popular products, such as orange juice or mayonnaise.

• Shop the store brands whenever possible. Anymore, store brands have the same quality and flavor as name brands, and even the packaging is becoming more attractive, with colors and pictures instead of the former black-and-white generic boxes of the 1970s.

What is more, a number of store brands are supplied by the big name companies, like Bordon, Dole, H.J. Heinz, Ralston-Purina and Campbell. So by buying store brands you can get quality and quantity without all the cost which goes into advertising name brands.

At the beginning of the 20th century, people went to different stores for different food items. You went to the butcher for meat, the dry goods store for flour and sugar—it was all simple. You knew the store owners and probably you remained a customer at their stores your entire life.

It's not nearly so easy today, with supermarkets, computerization, and thousands of items to choose from. That doesn't mean it has to be overwhelming. As long as you keep your wits about you and remember that supermarkets want to make a profit as much as any other business, you can become a smart shopper who brings home bargains every week.

TURN YOUR HOBBIES INTO A BIG BUSINESS

When you pursue your hobbies and interests, do you get so caught up in them that time disappears? Do you live for the times when you can get together with others who have similar interests and talk about your hobbies? Do you wish you could work on your hobbies all of the time?

If you answered "yes" to these questions, you are a prime candidate for starting your own business centered around your favorite interests. The chances of your success as a business person are much greater if your business includes something for which you have a burning passion.

Basing a business on a hobby is not for the light-hearted dabbler—you have to feel deeply committed to your hobby to make it work. If you take out your carpenter tools four times a year to make cute little wooden toys for your grandchildren, you can pretty much forget about creating a business for yourself out of carpentry.

The perfect candidate for a hobby-based business is a person who spends most of his spare time in deep involvement with his craft. This person not only works at a hobby, but he also studies it from every angle. The born enthusiast will understand all the products and services used in the hobby, as well as all the problems hobbyists face obtaining certain necessities.

• Advantages

The advantages you have in starting a business based on a hobby include knowing enough about your fellow enthusiasts to understand their tastes and follow the developments in the hobby, being able to come up with a creative idea which will appeal to your target group, and having enough contacts in the world of your hobby to get guinea pigs to test your product.

• What constitutes a great business idea

A great business idea capitalizes on an unusual, hard-to-find angle. It is okay if you like to make stuffed animals for your children, but it doesn't become a business until you can develop patterns for stuffed animals which are dressed up to resemble Charles Dickens' characters. In this case, you can make money both by selling the patterns and by creating finished dolls.

The important thing is find your niche—and stay there. Don't try to cover every angle of your hobby or you will get lost. Concentrate on finding steady customers for the one or two items you can provide. And have fun learning more about your hobbies, as well as meeting new people who are just as excited as you are.

• How to break into the business

The biggest problem you will face in developing your hobby into a business is finding ways to distribute your product. Here are some potential places:
√ Advertising in hobbyists' publications. Every hobby has at least one magazine or bulletin.
√ Obtaining mail order lists compiled by hobbyists' associations.
√ Putting your product into specialized stores which concentrate on your hobby.
√ Advertising on Compuserve's hobby forum on your computer.

√ Finding fellow hobbyists in other parts of the country who are willing to advocate the use of your product.
√ Obtaining a free listing in the Crafters Quest Directory. This is for people who want to sell crafts to stores or to other crafters. Send a long, self-addressed, stamped envelope to: The Front Room, Dept. CCD, Box 1541, Clifton, NJ 07015-1541 for information.

Your interests don't have to be unusual in order to make them pay off for you. They can range from collecting paperback books to making picture frames out of old tree stumps. You can even turn a love for animals into a thriving business.

PET SITTING

For most people, Fido and Fluffy become so much a part of the family, that they will do almost anything to avoid putting their pets into kennels during out-of-town trips. This is where a pet sitting service is a gold mine.

By hiring a pet sitter, an animal owner makes sure their pets stay in their normal environment and receive their meals at regular times. When they hire you as a sitter, pet owners pay for someone who will check on their animals two or three times a day, feed them, play with the cats for half an hour, and walk the dogs. The pet owner also gets the added benefits of having someone around who can bring the mail into the house and turn lights off and on, thereby scaring off burglars.

• Income and expenditures

The average pet sitter charges $10 per visit for a cat and $12 per visit for a dog, with a $5 charge for each additional animal after that. When you make two or three trips a day, the money can really add up. Once your business gets established, you can make $3,000 to $6,000 a month. And people will pay those prices. Without you, they would be paying around $40 to kennel their pets in a disturbing environment where they stand a chance of contracting some infectious disease.

Your expenditures include some toys for the dogs and cats, money spent on gas while making your rounds, and perhaps a few dollars to advertise in the want-ads of your local paper.

The work is steady, because once you become a trusted pet sitter, your clients will call you again and again. In fact, you will become such a necessity that people will begin planning their vacations around your schedule! Your busiest times will be vacation seasons, such as summer and holidays.

• The daily schedule

It is wise to accept only as many jobs as you can handle in a day. If you are the only one working, this means about six customers a day.

The first shift begins at about 7 a.m., when you walk all of the dogs and check on other animals. You should be done by 10 a.m. You are free until the second shift starts at 3 p.m., at which time you walk and play with the animals, and probably feed them. The second shift ends around 6 p.m. Your last visit begins at 10 p.m., when you let dogs out for a last 5-minute run.

The nice thing about pet sitting is the whole family can get in on the act. You can be walking the dog while your daughter plays with the cat and your spouse checks on another animal client. If you find you have plenty of customers and your family doesn't get involved, hire some extra people.

• Other potential pet businesses

If the thought of moving around in a stranger's house doesn't appeal to you, set up another business geared to pet owners. For example, put together a daily dog-walking service, or open a pet-accessory business, a grooming business, or an obedience training school. You can even establish a vet transport service, or a pet-food delivery service.

The key to making a success out of your hobby or interest is to capitalize on your strengths. If you know what you like, chances are you will find someone who needs what you have to offer.

10 STEPS TO GREATER CREATIVITY

Have you ever finished a fantastic book and wondered how the author could possibly have invented all the ideas that went into it? Or perhaps there is someone at work who somehow imagines ways to solve problems which no one else ever considered. How do these people do it?

The answer is that they use their creativity. You don't have to be a writer, a composer, or an artist to be creative. You simply need to be able to look at the world with new eyes and use what you see in new ways. No matter what you do for a living or how old you are, you can increase your creativity and make it work for you. The steps to better creativity are:

• Think about yourself and your past

You will be amazed at how much this will open up your mind to new ideas. By thinking about your experiences, you can uncover new facts or new relationships among different data you've collected, which might lead to greater ideas. Also, you can rid yourself of any inhibitions about creativity you might have buried in your past. Maybe a teacher or sibling told you once that you had the creativity of an old shoe, and you believed him. That opinion of yourself is not true and you don't have to accept it.

• Don't get trapped in a role

If you select a defined role, such as the businessman with the conservative three-piece suit, you might find it harder to break away and become the Picasso of the board room. Leave yourself open and flexible.

• Think like a child

Have you ever sat on a hillside, looked up at the sky, and wondered what it would be like to travel faster than any human ever has before? Well, you are not alone. According to legend, Albert Einstein discovered the theory of relativity by imagining himself flying at the speed of light. If imagination worked for such a distinguished scientist, it can also work for you.

Children thrive on large doses of imagination. It allows them to see the world in new ways, and to try different activities. In order to open up your own imagination, do something you've never done before but always wondered about, or just sit and daydream. When you release your mind from the confines of everyday life, you leave yourself open to all manner of fresh ideas.

• Write down all your ideas
Otherwise known as brainstorming, this procedure allows you to explore all aspects of a particular project or problem. Don't worry if your ideas seem far-fetched or crazy—just get some ideas on paper. You can judge them for soundness at a later time.

• Confront your frustrations
Sometimes it seems that no matter what you do, the creative juices simply won't flow. Just don't sit there and stew about it, confront it. See if you can figure out what is stopping your creativity, and then write about it. This will help free up the creative flow.

• Change your surroundings
If you still have trouble being creative, change something about your environment—go to another room, take a walk, change your clothes, or maybe do a few chores. Sometimes it helps to get away from the problem entirely for awhile by imagining yourself somewhere you would really like to visit.

• Analyze your ideas
Now is the time to review your ideas and see if any of them have potential.

• Don't worry about making mistakes
Failure happens to the best of us. It is a well-known fact that Einstein did poorly in school, was fired from his first job, even his doctoral dissertation—the theory of relativity—was rejected by his university. But he never gave up. If you fail, figure out what didn't work, and then try again. Write out your ideas in great detail, look for the flaws in your thinking, and then try to come up with more creative ideas.

• There is no excuse for not being creative
It doesn't matter if you are 80-years-old, crippled, or completely lacking in spare time, you can still be creative. Pablo Picasso

continued to paint and draw into his 90s. The poet William Carlos Williams published three books of his poetry between ages 68 and 79, despite having suffered a stroke that left him paralyzed. If you don't have free time, then be creative on the job.

• Live with encouragers, not discouragers
If a friend or family member tries to discourage you creative efforts by telling you your ideas will never work, find people to associate with who will support your efforts.

Creative thinking is not just one method of climbing the ladder of success—it is a way of life. When you open up your mind to the potential for new ideas, you learn the joys of exploring, experimenting, and figuring things out for yourself. You learn how to live.

INVENT YOUR WAY TO SUCCESS

Do you have an idea for a new invention or an improvement on an existing product? If so, you are not alone. Many people dream of being the next Alexander Graham Bell or Thomas Edison, and they feel their ideas can be million dollar money-makers—if only they knew how to market their inventions.

The interesting thing is marketing an invention is not as complicated as you might think. You just have to know the process to go through to get your product from its present spot as a small kernel of an idea at the back of your mind to store shelves across the country. The steps to marketing your invention are as follows:

(1) Document your idea
Before you do anything else, buy a notebook with numbered pages and start keeping a detailed, dated diary of your idea as it develops. This is a good way to prove you had an idea first if a quetion ever arises at the U.S. Patent Office or in court.

You can also document your idea with the U.S. Patent Office's Document Disclosure Program. Send two copies of a written description of your idea, two copies of drawings or photographs of your concept, and a $10 check, to Document Disclosure Program; U.S. Patent and Trademark Office; Washington, D.C. 20231. Although it isn't a patent, registering your idea gives you official proof in a court of law.

If your idea has a distinctive look, like a new game board or clothing design, you should also file for a copyright. To learn more about the copyrighting process, write to the Registrar of Copyrights; Copyright Office; Library of Congress; Washington, D.C. 20559 and request the free booklets Publications on Copyrights and Copyright Basics.

(2) Do your homework
Check out your friends, relatives, catalogs, and local stores. You want to make sure no one else has already marketed a product quite like yours. Perhaps something is on the market which is similar to your idea. In that case, is there something unique about your idea which will make it even better than the current available product? Also, find out what other businesses charge for similar products and make an estimate of how much to charge for your product which is competitive with the existing market.

Show several friends and relatives rough sketches of your invention and question them about the usefulness of your product.

The specific questions to focus on are:
· Do you need this product?
· If it were on the market, would you buy this product?
· How much would you pay for this product?
These are three very important questions. If no one feels he needs your product, now is a good time to find out before you spend any more money. You can also discover if your cost estimate is reasonable in the eyes of potential future customers.

(3) Design and build a model
Next, you need to draw a formal blueprint of your invention, showing exact dimensions and listing the materials you will use to make a working model. The drawing needs to be complete and accurate so that someone in a machine shop can construct the prototype model, but it doesn't have to look like a professional engineer put it together. If you don't feel artistic enough to make your own drawing, hire a student from a design school, or even from your local high school's drafting class, to create the drawing.

Don't be surprised if you have to make several adjustments

in your drawing, adding or subtracting features. The more work you do now, the better your model will be.

After the drawing is completed to your satisfaction, it's time to build the prototype or first model of your invention. Once again, if you don't feel qualified to construct the model, hire a talented local shop student at the high school, or visit a model car or railroad trade show, where you will meet people who put together prototypes as a hobby. You can also check the phone book and get names of local machine shops or model makers, if you want a truly professional model. Make sure, however, that you get estimates on the cost before any work is done!

(4) Test your product
Put your invention through a series of test runs, and make notes of its good and bad points. Also give the model to a few trusted friends or relatives and see how it works in an everyday environment. Now is the time to work out the bugs, if possible.

Now is the time also to make sure you make a notation in your notebook, signed and dated by a witness, that you have created a working model. This is an important step in establishing yourself as the original inventor.

You are now in a position to do one of three things. You can apply for a patent and go into business manufacturing your invention yourself. A second choice is to sell your idea outright to an interested company. Finally, you can negotiate a license agreement with a company whereby you're paid a minimum annual payment, or royalty, for the use of your idea.

(5) Manufacture your invention yourself
• Make between 50 and 200 copies of your model and sell them in a few stores. Talk to the store managers and arrange to sell the product on a consignment basis. That way, the managers aren't stuck with a product which won't sell.

This is a good way to prove to potential investors that your invention is a good risk.

• Run a few small ads in your local paper, or offer to split the cost of advertising with the stores. Do what you can to bring people into the store to buy your product.

This is the moment of truth for your idea, because it shows once and for all whether people are interested enough in your product to buy it. If your invention doesn't sell fast enough, you either forget the whole thing before it costs you even more money, or you literally go back to the drawing board, do more market research, and make adjustments on your model.

• Have someone with a desk-top printer produce a three-color, illustrated one page flier which describes the success you had test marketing your product. Distribute copies of your flier to industry insiders and key contacts as you work to arrange monetary backing for a much larger production of your invention.

• Continue to produce copies of your invention on your own as you work to gain the interests of a larger corporation. This shows your potential investors that you have faith in your product. It also establishes a track record for your invention.

As your sales increase, begin marketing your product in other regional stores. When your markets are solid in a region, start thinking about marketing nationally.

6) Sell your idea outright
Another option is to sell your idea or invention outright to a company that already manufactures products similar to your own. When you sell outright, you present the company with a bill for services rendered plus any expenses. Say you charge $100 an hour, you worked a total of 60 hours, and you used $4,000 in materials. Your total gain on your invention would be $10,000. Once you get your check, you are no longer responsible for your invention, nor are you able to share in the profits.

7) Negotiate a licensing agreement
When you negotiate a licensing agreement, you are asking to share in the profits from the manufacture and sale of your invention.   In a minimum payment/royalty sale, you receive a percentage, usually around five percent, of the invoice cost of each product sold.

What is more, at the beginning of each year while you hold the contract, the company pays you a minimum against these royalties, usually around 50 percent of projected annual royalties. What this means is that if the company projects an annual sale of $100,000 at five percent per product, your total annual royalty will be $50,000, with the company paying you $25,000 in one lump sum at the beginning of the year!

The beauty of inventing is that you don't have to tackle really big projects, like a car that runs on distilled water, in order to make money. Many money-making inventions start out with someone wanting to create a solution to some small problem in his or her environment.

Look around you! Perhaps you can put together an invention which tells people when their house plants need to be watered, or something which automatically throws away junk mail, or a new way to peel a carrot, or even a better mouse trap! Many times your invention makes improvements on existing products. Check household and kitchen gadgets for ways you can improve them.

Inventing can be that spare time hobby which ends up making you some very nice pocket change.

MARITAL FINANCES

One of the biggest causes of marital arguments and divorces is finances. He spends too much on his friends, or he doesn't give me enough money to buy groceries; she is altogether too tight-fisted, or she has "shop till you drop" printed across her forehead. These are all common complaints which can come to the surface at any time in a marriage.

The important thing to remember is arguments over money do not have to put a brick wall between you and your spouse. In fact a good argument can be healthy for a marriage because it can get wants, wishes, and worries out in the open where they can be dealt with by the couple. However, there are some crucial rules to remember when dealing with the family finances. They are:

• You married your spouse for better or for worse, so treat your mate with respect. A discussion over money is no time to assign blame, call names, poke fun, or rant and rave. Being nice to one another will get you much farther along on the road to solving your true problem.

• Figure out a budget on which you can both agree. Don't run your house like a session of Congress, but rather do what compromising is necessary to make progress.

• Share in the decisions. Even if only one of you actually brings in the paycheck, you should both decide how to spend it. If you don't, one spouse is relegated to second-class citizenship in the marriage and may end up feeling resentful and angry.

• Discuss your family finances at least once a month. For many people, finances is the hardest topic to talk about. It's even harder to talk about than sex. Get used to the idea of discussion and use your time wisely to go over the family budget, plan purchases, and decide your future goals. When you do decide to talk about money, stick to the point, and don't drag in other marital problems.

• Avoid making large purchases without input from both members of the couple. Perhaps you agree to discuss any purchase over $50 before you actually make it.

• Make sure you are mentally ready to discuss finances. If you feel tired or upset, you might be more inclined to argue. If you do get into an argument, use logic, not emotion, to carry your opinions.

• If there is something about the way your spouse spends money that annoys you, be direct. Talk about it and see if a compromise can't be worked out. If you don't discuss the problems, you stew on them and finance time becomes a battleground.

• Don't compare your financial situation with anyone else. It doesn't solve your problems and can lead to feelings of resentment.

• When the time comes to pay the bills, share the responsibility. That way both of you know where the money goes and where you stand financially.

• Accept the fact that you might not win every argument. That is what compromising is all about.

• If your finances become such a serious problem that you can't ever seem to cooperate or decide anything, seek help. Find a credit counselor who can help you put together a budget and learn how to successfully handle your money. It might not hurt to make arrangements for a marriage counselor also, to iron out your unresolved issues.

Put your marriage first. Accept the fact that you aren't always going to get your way. By continually arguing, you can put a rift in your marriage that you won't be able to fix.

NATURAL TREATMENTS FOR MEMORY LOSS

Many people suffer a certain amount of memory loss, especially what is known as short-term memory loss. Try remembering the names of 20 or 30 new acquaintances at a conference. Probably by the next week, you won't recall the names of more than 10 of them, unless there was something distinctive about each one. Just remembering where you left your car keys is sometimes a real chore.

Recent studies have shown that treatment with certain vitamins, herbs, and other food extracts can improve your memory, your alertness, and slow the effects of aging. Some natural products can even increase your IQ! Doctors have started prescribing the addition of these nutrients to their patients' diets to reverse memory loss due to senility. Many of the memory stimulating vitamins and herbs are available at your local health food store. Among the more familiar natural treatments are:

CHOLINE—This is a substance necessary for the production of acetylcholine, which is an extremely important neurotransmitter involved in memory and learning.

GOTU KOLA—This natural stimulant increases mental alertness without the side-effects caused by caffeine.

LECITHIN—Like Choline, it may increase the level of neurotransmitters in your brain. It might also improve your ability to learn.

PHENYLALANINE—This amino acid is used in the manufacture of norepinephrine, a chemical that stimulates your brain cells.

PYRIDOXINE (VITAMIN B6)—Pyridoxine is an antioxidant which works with other nutrients.

RNA (RIBONUCLEIC ACID)—This natural substance is considered to be a memory source molecule. Researchers believe that loss of RNA in your later years may be responsible for loss of memory capacity.

Many people who use the natural substances notice an improvement in their memory and alertness in a very short time.

Another naturally occurring substance which has proven to increase mental performance in lab tests is ginkgo-biloba extract. Tests show that people who use the extract over a period of time show a significant improvement in their short-term memory after the first six weeks, and an equally noticeable improvement in their learning rate after 24 weeks!

For those of you who prefer a prescription drug to help enhance your mental abilities, there is Eldepryl. This drug stimulates your short-term memory by inhibiting your body's production of the enzyme monoamine oxidase (MAO). MAO lowers the level of dopamine—an extremely important neurotransmitter which is critical to immune function, physical energy, short-term memory, and sexual desire. Usually after age 45, the level of dopamine in the brain drops 13 percent every decade. Eldepryl protects your brain from this natural decline, thereby maintaining your short-term memory at its pre-45-age level.

SURGERY: WHAT YOU SHOULD KNOW AND DO

Entering a hospital can be a frightening, nerve-wracking experience for anyone. You don't really know what to expect, and the nagging question of whether you really need the surgery after all remains at the back of your mind.

It is extremely important to ask your doctor or surgeon questions about your upcoming treatment, both to set your own mind at rest and to show the medical personnel that you are interested in what happens to you. After all, you are the most important person in a surgery situation, and all your energies should be focused on getting well instead of worrying.

But what questions should you ask? To whom should you ask these questions? The following is a list of questions you have a right to have answered before you ever agree to surgery:

WHAT TO ASK YOUR DOCTOR

Are there any alternatives to this surgery?

This is good to ask for any surgery, because sometimes alternatives exist which may be just as effective, but don't require surgery. A good example is Caesareans. Four out of five Caesareans are unnecessary. They cost more than natural birth and require more recovery time.

Another example is the temporary pacemaker that surgeons usually implant during cardiac surgery. A non-invasive pacemaker with electrodes attached outside the chest doesn't require as much surgery and is proven effective in 94 percent of patients.

Always get a second opinion, especially if you aren't quite comfortable with your doctor's answer. Almost 80 percent of some procedures may not be recommended by a second doctor. When you have conflicting medical opinions, feel free to see a third or even a fourth doctor. The more you know, the more comfortable you will be with the surgery.

Have you had a lot of experience with this procedure?

Research indicates that the more a physician performs certain procedures, the better he becomes. However, it is also important to choose a surgeon who keeps on top of the latest information in his field. New and better ways to handle old problems are constantly being developed. For instance, an up-to-date surgeon probably would not perform a Halsted mastectomy, because more modern technologies are now available.

Another item that could be important to check is the credentials of your surgeon, especially if you don't know the person. You can do this by talking with your state's medical association. It might surprise you to learn that some "surgicenters" may legally employ surgeons who are not board certified. And on rare occasions, a non-qualified doctor does slip through the cracks in the system. This does not mean you should mistrust all doctors. For every bad doctor, there are dozens of wonderful, caring physicians who work hard to do it right.

How much will this procedure cost?

Get the cost of the surgery in writing from the doctor, not the nurse or secretary, before it actually occurs. And remember— fees are often negotiable! You can save a great deal of money by having a formal agreement on charges before the day of surgery.

WHAT TO ASK THE HOSPITAL

What are your in-hospital infection rates?

About 10 percent of patients develop an infection during their stay in a hospital. This is usually the result of flaws in hospital sanitation procedures. If the hospital won't give you the figures, ask your doctor. Any hospital with an in-hospital infection rate of around five percent is doing a good job with their sanitation. Remember: half of all in-hospital infections can be prevented by the hospital personnel washing their hands. It may not hurt to pleasantly remind the personnel to wash up.

What kind of training and experience does the supporting surgical staff have?

Ask to meet your anesthesiologist and the certified nurse anesthetist. Find out what they will be doing throughout the entire surgery. It is crucial to know the anesthesiologist's credentials in an outpatient setting—whether in the hospital's outpatient department, the doctor's office, or an independent surgery center. He should be board certified in anesthesiology, not just board eligible.   Also, everyone on the surgical staff should know CPR.

How do you deal with emergencies?

You especially need to ask this question if you are scheduled for non-hospital surgery. You need to know whether the outpatient or surgery center has an ambulance on standby to transport emergency patients, and whether there is a written agreement with a local hospital to take emergency patients immediately. Sometimes non-hospital patients are routed through the emergency room instead of being immediately accepted into the hospital.

How often do you do this procedure?

Once again, the more practice a surgeon and a medical facility have in treating patients who have experienced your procedure, the better off you are. For example, recovery rates for coronary bypass surgery increase dramatically when a hospital does 100 or more bypasses in a year.

WHAT TO ASK THE ANESTHESIOLOGIST

What kind of anesthesia will you use?

The anesthesiologist can choose between local (anesthesia that works on a small portion of a body, like a finger), regional (this numbs a larger part of the body, like the abdominal area), or general anesthetics (which puts you completely to sleep). Find out which type the anesthesiologist will use and why.

How will the anesthesia affect me?

Ask the anesthesiologist to explain to you exactly what will happen to you as the anesthesia takes effect, what happens while you are under anesthesia, and what to expect as you begin to come out from under the influence of the anesthesia.

By asking these questions, you show your medical staff that you are knowledgeable and care about what is going to happen to you during surgery. You will probably become an individual to them instead of just another number on a chart. Studies show that patients who get involved and ask questions about their surgery receive above average treatment from their medical staff.

WRITING AN EFFECTIVE RESUME

Whether you are entering the job market right out of college or re-entering after a period of time, the best way to handle a job application is to construct a resume. With a resume, you have an opportunity to convince a potential employer that you are different from others and the best one for the job. A resume can be a calling card and professional history all wrapped up into one package. It also reminds your potential employer of who you are long after an interview is over.

Resume writing can be a frightening experience for anyone who hasn't done it before. After all, it can be the only thing which stands between you and an interview for a great new job! But as long as you can accept some dos and don'ts connected with resume writing, and follow a certain pattern, you, too, can put together a very professional-looking resume which shouts out: "I'm perfect for the job! Hire me!"

THE DOS AND DON'TS OF RESUME WRITING

Don'ts

• Do not ever ever write a lie or half-truth on your resume! This cannot be stressed enough. The only way your potential employer can judge you is from what you put on your resume. If you put even one fib on your resume, an embarrassing question during an interview can expose you as a liar and ruin your chances for the job.

For example, say your grandmother makes money on the side by baking cookies for the neighbors. Don't turn a week's worth of cleaning pantry shelves into "Reorganized professional baker's business" on your resume. At the interview, your future boss might ask you how you managed a major reorganization, since that is exactly what she's planning on doing in the near future.

• Don't put anything negative into your resume. Because you are trying to sell yourself, emphasize the positive and call attention to your strengths.

• Don't ramble or use long, complicated sentences in your resume. Employers have very little time to look at resumes. If a future employer has to take time to figure out what you are trying to say, chances are he won't get beyond the first line and your resume will end up in the circular file. Instead, get to the point immediately, avoid using "I" or "me," and concentrate on putting action verbs, like coordinated, negotiated, managed, or developed, into your resume.

It's okay to use partial sentences on resumes, as long as you get your point across. For example, if you were in charge of festivities for your town's annual apple-picker day celebration, you could list this on your resume followed by the description "Organized annual festival for hometown."

• Do not let your resume grow to be more than one-and-one-half pages at the most. This might mean you don't list every job or part-time job you've ever had. Concentrate instead on any job which has particular relevance to the position for which you are applying. Not only does this go a long way toward convincing a potential employer you are experienced enough for the job, but it also shows you know how to sift through all the information and find only the facts which apply. This shows common sense and good organizational skills—two items employers are always searching for when they look at resumes.

• Do not leave even one word misspelled on a resume or a cover letter. If you have to, hire somebody to proof your writing. You might have the best organized and most fascinating resume ever to cross a desk, but nothing turns an employer off faster than a misspelled word. Such an item seriously calls into question either your education and intelligence levels, or your personal habits of neatness.

The Dos

• Be specific about jobs, dates, locations, and any description of the skills you acquired. Also, if you have to fill out an application, make sure the dates and information matches what you say on your resume.

• Make sure you include critical information, such as your name, address, and phone number at the top of your resume.

• Rewrite your resume as many times as it takes to make it perfect in your eyes. Then show it to other people for suggestions on how to make it even better.

• Leave some white space on the resume. It shouldn't look like you copied a page out of a book. Instead, leave extra space between sections, and indent whenever necessary. You want to make it easy to read in a minute or two.

• If you are interested in more than one type of position in a company, make sure you put together separate resumes for each job. Unless it's a very small business, each resume will come to the attention of different supervisors. If you try to pack everything you want to do in a company onto one resume, it will look like you don't know exactly what you want in a job.

You may also find after a self-evaluation that you are interested in more than one professional area. Make up individual resumes for each area you wish to pursue.

PRE-RESUME WRITING

Sometimes it helps to do a little self-evaluation before you tackle the specifics which go into your resume. Take the time to think about what you want in a job, what your personal strengths are, and whether your "ideal" job is actually right for you.

Ask yourself questions like:

• Am I self-directed or do I need supervision in order to get my work done?
• Am I comfortable with repetition or do I need constant change and

challenges to be happy?
• Do I prefer the closeness of a small business to the anonymity of a large corporation?
• Can I keep my head and sense of humor in a crisis?
• Is salary the most important thing I am looking for in a job?
• Do I postpone problems rather than solve them?
• Can I think through projects far in advance and come up with creative and resourceful solutions?

If you have a particular job in mind, write down why you feel you would be particularly good at it and why someone should hire you to do it.

THE RESUME

• Name, address, telephone number(s).
These should be at the very top of your resume, where your future employer can easily refer to them.

• Jobs and description.
List your jobs in order from the most recent to the furthest past. Include Name of company and supervisor, date of employment, address, and brief description of position held or skills used.

• Education.
If you've had any post-high school education, write down the name of the university or college, your major(s), and any degrees you obtained. Like the job section, write these in order starting with the most recent. If you recently graduated from college, the education section should go before the job section on your resume.

• Other.
If you still have room, you can briefly list interesting hobbies, outside interests, volunteer activities, or any special traveling you've done, like that trip to England (as long as it has some bearing on the job in question). Items like these can make you stand out in a crowd.

• Willing to relocate.
If you are willing to move in order to get a job, say so. For some companies, that is a very desirable quality. A willingness to move also shows you are extremely interested in working for the company.

• References.

This part of your resume should say, "Available upon request." That doesn't mean you shouldn't have at least three references in mind; instead you should avoid listing your references' names and addresses on your resume. If a potential employer is interested in you, you can bet he or she will ask for references and check them.

Always ask a person if you can use him or her for a reference. Otherwise, you might choose someone who doesn't really know you and who can give you a lukewarm reference at best.

HOW THE RESUME LOOKS

You want your resume to look as professional as possible. If you have the money, your best bet is to go to a printer and have and have a number of resumes printed professionally. If you decide to do it yourself, throw your old typewriter in the corner and borrow a friend's word processor.

If possible, use a laser printer to make a number of original quality copies. When forced to use a copy machine, find a good one that doesn't leave a lot of black specks on your resume. You want every copy to look as good as the original.

When you choose your paper, don't try to stand out too much. Avoid neon colors at all cost. Choose eight-and-one-half by 11 inch rag bond paper with a 20- to 24-pound stock and a 25 percent cotton content. The best colors are ivory, antique tan, a very pale gray, ice blue, or white.

THE COVER LETTER

When you send your resume through the mail, you need to add a cover letter. The cover letter should not be longer than one page. Like the resume, it should be specific, with short, active verb sentences.

You use the cover letter to explain anything which didn't fit within your resume. It usually includes the following:

• An explanation as to why you wrote the letter, such as in response to a newspaper advertisement or inquiry to possible openings.

• An explanation as to why you are interested in employment at the company.

• Highlights of specific work experience with a reference to your resume for further study.

• Your desire for an interview, along with a mention that you will make a follow-up call at a specific time, such as 10 days.

When you write a cover letter, make sure you address it to a specific person by name. If you don't, your resume might bounce from desk to desk without anyone reading it.

Resumes are as individual in looks as the people who write them. For most employers, the resume is the first chance they have of meeting you. Let your resume reflect who you are and what you are capable of doing.

Will I Lose My Job?

With companies struggling for financial survival and no job seemingly safe anymore, you probably find yourself frequently worrying about exactly how safe your job is. Because of cutbacks, streamlining, and the continual introduction of new technology, everyone with a job from assembly line worker to the president of a major corporation has the potential to find himself standing in an unemployment line.

How do you figure out if your job is the next in line to get the ax? Better yet, how do you prevent yourself from becoming a victim of change in your company? Even if you work hard with a smaller support staff and you seem busier than ever, it never hurts to continually improve your position so that you become invaluable to your company.

The key is to always keep your eyes and ears open to what goes on around you. Often people don't pay attention to potential job loss because they don't want to accept that it might happen. Be a realist—pay attention to the signs that your job is about to be discontinued.

WARNING SIGNS THAT THE AX IS FALLING

• You are being left out of company communication.
This could cover anything from not having access to informal information and losing your grip on the grapevine, to being left out of your supervisors official announcements and meetings.

• You or your department is falling back on production.
You might have lost a few accounts or realized that somehow you aren't producing as many products as you once were.

• An outsider is called in.
Many companies find it difficult to fire or lay-off their own people, especially if the employees have been with the company for a long time. Often they call in a consultant, whose job it is to study the situation and make recommendations on changes—including who to fire. If you see a grim, non-sociable stranger hanging around studying your work, watch out! He could be deciding your future.

You don't have to wait for the ax to fall, however. Start immediately trying to improve your skills and developing connections within your organization. Even if you do lose your present job, the network of people you develop now might help you get and keep a different job. Here are some strategies on how to safeguard your job:

• Actively gather information.
Go the extra mile to research ideas and problems with which your company deals. Study journals and conference reports, talk to experts in the field and others in your industry, and brainstorm on ways to handle situations differently. Talk to your superiors about any new ideas or different approaches which come out of your research. By staying on top of current research in your industry, you have a good idea where the jobs are if you do lose your job.

• Think creatively about ways to generate business.
Look at old ideas and work to expand them, or call on old clients. Perhaps you could even work on ideas to expand the company into areas no one has explored before.

• Analyze the past.
Look at past deals or products on which the company lost money,

and analyze what went wrong. Then figure out ways for preventing this from happening in the future.

• Strengthen your relationship with your boss.
Get to know him or her to the point where you feel comfortable approaching your boss with new ideas. Imagine that the whole company's future rides on what you can accomplish in the next few weeks, and keep your boss informed on your activities. This can make you stand out in a crowd.

• Use the Golden Rule with your boss.
Your boss is a human being and likes to be treated with respect. However, some employees, for fear of appearing too eager, end up rudely ignoring their bosses except to take orders. It would probably make you feel uncomfortable if you were ignored, and the same is true with your boss.

If your boss does a good job handling a difficult problem, let him or her know you genuinely admire the effort. The trick is to be sincere in your praise. Find an opportunity to ask your boss what his or her future plans are for the company, and then ask what you can do to help. Remember: people are your greatest assets. Treat them well.

• Expand your network of people.
Get to know people all along the chain of command. Study company bulletins and reports to see who is involved with what projects. That way, if you run into someone in the hall, parking lot, or elevator, you can discuss projects and ideas with him or her.

• Build morale in your own department.
If your department accomplishes something ahead of schedule, treat them to an outing or informal party. Get to know the people you work with on a social level. If nothing else, you might find out who is having problems at work and help them along.

• Improve your skills.
Any additional education you acquire is a step in the right direction. Besides reading or researching on your own, take business or computer courses at your local college or university, or work toward a degree. Perhaps you discover your company plans on expanding its markets into Germany.

Take some courses in the German language so you are prepared for the future.

• Enrich your personal life.
Nobody can work forever at a job without having an outlet for stress. By starting new projects in your personal life, you give yourself time to relax. A relaxed person makes a much better employee than one who is stressed out. Get involved with the boy scouts or 4-H, build a cabinet or sew a quilt, write a book— whatever makes you feel comfortable.

If you lose your job anyway, you may think all of this is a waste of time, but it's not. Many people find new doors open for them which they never imagined while at their old job. Sometimes, connections you made among your superiors can pay off as they recommend you for positions because you are knowledgeable, hard-working, and trustworthy.

This may be a great opportunity to rethink your career and decide whether you might not want to try something different. Maybe you'll even decide to start your own business. It is your life, and the more you take control of it, the better off you will be.

SAVE MONEY ON YOUR TRAVELS

Whether you travel on vacation or for business, it always gives you a good feeling when you find special ways to save money. Many tricks exist for getting the most out of your travel dollar. Here are some tips for stretching your dollars on airlines, in hotels, car rentals, travel clubs, and time-shares.

AIRLINE FARES

You can save 50 to 75 percent on your airline fares by using loopholes and the airline industry's gray market. Remember: not all of the following suggestions are completely acceptable to airline companies.

• Hidden city fares
The best way to explain hidden city fares is to use an example. Let us say that you live in Sacramento, California and you want to go to Chicago to visit your mother. A direct plane ticket from Sacramento

to Chicago costs $620. At the same time, a plane ticket from Sacramento to St. Louis, with a stopover in Chicago costs $460. You buy the Sacramento to St. Louis ticket, and stop in Chicago without flying the extra miles to St. Louis. By doing this, you have just saved yourself $160.

Although there is nothing illegal about this maneuver, the airline industry frowns upon it because they lose an estimated millions of dollars every year when passengers use hidden fares or back-to-back tickets to save money.

• Back-to-back ticketing.
This tactic is very popular among passengers who use the airlines frequently. With back-to-back ticketing, a passenger buys two round-trip tickets from, say, Minneapolis to St. Louis for $300 apiece, with each ticket requiring a Saturday night layover.

The passenger uses alternate halves of each set of tickets to avoid the layover, while still paying less than the normal fare for a mid-week round-trip, which might cost $1,000.

• Plan ahead.
Several airlines give early-bird discounts to people who make their reservations months in advance.

• Be flexible.
If possible, plan to fly whichever airline gives you the best deal at whatever time of day or night. Also consider changing your departure or destination city in order to get a lower fare.

• Fly during off-peak days and off-peak hours.

• Travel on a holiday.
Most people aren't flying Thanksgiving Day, Christmas Day, or Easter Day.

• Travel during off-seasons.
Every destination has its time when fewer tourists visit. For areas around the world, they are—the Carribean: March through November; South America: April through November; Australia and New Zealand: April through August; Asia: January and February; and Europe: November through March.

· Check alternative agencies.
You can get tickets in places other than the normal travel agent or airline sources. Always pay for your ticket with a credit card if you use an alternative agency so you can get a refund, if necessary. Three alternative sources are:

√ Consolidators or Discount Agencies.
Consolidators handle large numbers of passengers. Because they receive large commissions from the airlines they work with, they often give their customers large 20 to 40 percent discounts. Consolidators usually specialize in one particular region or country.

Consolidators can waive advance purchase requirements and minimum- and maximum-stay limits. Some reliable consolidatorsare:

* Council Travel, (415-421-3473 in San Francisco) or (212-254-2525 in New York).

* Cut Rate Travel, (800-388-0575 or 708-405-0575).
* Euram Tours, (800-848-6789 or 202-789-2255).

* Getaway Travel (800-683-6336 or 305-446-7855).

*TFI Tours International Ltd., (212-736-1140 or 800-745-8000).

* Tickets & Tours, (212-697-7895).

* Unitravel, (800-325-2222 or 314-569-0900).

* Up and Away Travel Inc., (212-889-2345).

√ Bucket shops.
Bucket shops specialize in unsold tours and airline tickets. They are located in London, Amsterdam, Athens, Hong Kong, Singapore, Bangkok, and San Francisco. If you are looking for one, check the travel ads in newspapers of the cities listed above.

Although you can save up to two-thirds on your ticket, you have to be careful when dealing with bucket shops. Most of them only take

cash, so don't have any opportunity to get a refund. Also, since many bucket shops are not bonded and licensed, cancellation penalties are high. The following bucket shops are located in London:
* Bestway Travel and Tours Ltd., 56/58 Whitcomb St., London WC2, (tel.- 44-71-930-3985).
* Latitude 40, 13 Beauchamp Place, Knightsbridge, London SW3 1NQ, (tel.-44-71-581-1861).
* Worldwide Cheap Travel, 254 Earls Court Road, London SW5 AD (tel.-44-71-373-6465).

√ Coupon brokers.
Coupon brokers specialize in buying up unused frequent flyer awards and reselling them to the public at very low prices. You can get as much as 75 percent off, even if you want to fly first or business class, or you plan to fly coach for a very long distance. For your money, you also can get a free stopover in an additional city, or even free hotel rooms and rental cars, if your coupon covers these items.

However, there are some catches to the deal. First, some coupons have expiration dates or holiday blackouts. Secondly, you have to plan ahead because it usually take five to six weeks to get a coupon reissued in your name. Thirdly, the coupons are good only for the issuing airline.

And finally, the airline industry does not look at coupon brokerage in a favorable light. In fact, if you are caught with one of these coupons, the airlines will not honor it. Here are some guidelines when dealing with coupon brokers and phone numbers for a few brokers in case you decide to try this route:
* Make sure the broker reissues the coupon in your name.
* Only deal with first class or business class coupons.
* Make sure you can get a refund from your broker in case the airline won't accept your ticket. If the coupon broker doesn't give refunds, go elsewhere.
* Do not tell any member of the airline staff how you got your ticket.
* Always pay with a credit card.
* Addresses:
   Air Line Coupon Company, (800-354-4489).
   International Air Coupon Exchange, (800-873-3443 or 303-756-8050).

Nesher Travel, (800-875-0100 or 617-621-0123).

CAR RENTALS

When you rent a car, a sub-compact car is the cheapest price available. Beware of the desk agent at car rental agencies. Often, the agent will try to talk you into upgrading your rental to a larger, more expensive vehicle. If you would feel more comfortable with a larger vehicle, take it. But remember, the larger vehicle will add at least $100 to your bill.

HOTEL RESERVATIONS

The best way to save money on hotel reservations is to avoid the popular 800 reservation numbers you see in hotel listings and ads. Instead, call the hotel directly to see if there are any special deals available. If you are a member of an organization which offers special hotel discounts, mention this fact to the hotel.

Another alternative is to request the hotel's corporate rate, which is usually available to anyone who asks for it. This can save you five to 10 percent off the published rate. Use your employer's corporate hotel rates even for personal trips, and stay at business hotels on weekends, because rates are discounted by as much as 50 percent. If nothing else, ask the clerk if any special rates are available as you check in. Avoid the items which make your bill skyrocket, such as room service, minibars, and telephones.

Other ways of saving money include using a discount reservation hotline. Discounters reserve large numbers of rooms at a volume discount and then pass on the savings to their customers. Call Quikbook (800-221-3531) or Hotel Reservations Network (800-964-6835) and tell them where you are going and what kind of room you want.

TRAVEL CLUBS

For a certain fee every year, you can join a travel club and save up to 50 percent at participating hotels, discount coupon books for certain shops, and 10 to 30 percent off of cruises and tours. Annual fees range from about $20 to $99.

One travel club in the medium price range is Infinet Travel Club (800-966-2582) of Melrose, Massachusetts. For $49 a year, you can use their full-service travel agency, get 50 percent off 4,200 hotels worldwide, get up to 50 percent off on cruises, and acquire guarantees on the lowest available air fares. When you call, ask about the $19 a year special mentioned in their direct mail letter.

GET THE MOST FROM A TIME-SHARE

The best way to take advantage of a time-share at a resort is not to be an original investor. Resort time-shares allow people to use a house, apartment, or condominium at popular resorts for a certain amount of time every year. The property is shared with several other time-share owners, and everyone is liable for maintenance costs.

The biggest problem with owning a time-share is they can be very expensive, especially if a person is talked into purchasing a share by a high-pressure salesman. Often, time-share owners find they can't afford their share, or that they do not have enough time to take advantage of it. This is where you come in.

If you are interested in buying a time-share at a popular resort in Hawaii, Florida, Hilton Head, or some other vacation mecca, don't bother with the resort's sponsor, the man who wants to sell a high priced time-share to you. Instead, seek out a desperate time-share owner and make an offer.

Often, you can pick up a tremendous bargain. For example, the time-share owner paid $10,000 for a week in a a one-room apartment at a Hilton Head, South Carolina resort in January. However, the owner's job doesn't allow him to get to Hilton Head much, and the annual $600 maintenance fee is wasted money.

If that owner is desperate enough, you can buy that time-share from him for as little as $3,000. Time-shares go for rock bottom prices because once someone owns them, the owner is legally stuck with his share until another buyer can be found. The original sponsor of the resort's time-shares washes his hands of the deal once all the shares are sold the first time.

The way to go about snagging a time-share bargain is to visit an area where you think you might like to vacation regularly. Once you've found an area you like, make sure the sponsor has all his time-shares sold, because he tries to sell them at a high price, and he isn't going to like an outsider coming in and significantly decreasing the prices.

If all the shares are sold, locate several owners who might like to sell and make them low offers. Shop around and make sure what you bid for is really what you want. Finally, you negotiate the price and sign the papers.

Don't spend much time negotiating with someone who fully expects to get a full return on his investment—he's not going to take a bargain price offer anyway. Besides, there are probably plenty of other attractive time-shares available in the area from which you can choose.

DEDUCT YOUR VACATION

After all the fun and adventure of your travels, there is still one more way you might be able to save some money—courtesy of the IRS.

Whether you can deduct for your travel expenses or not depends on whether the trip was primarily business or pleasure.

• The IRS allows you to deduct money spent for business, but not for pleasure trips. Say you have a business meeting in Atlanta which lasts for four days, and then you spend three more days visiting friends who live there. The money spent for four days of business is deductible, but not the three extra days.

• If your trip is primarily business, you can deduct travel expenses, but you have to allocate the other expenses, like meals and hotels. For example, costs for the four business days in Atlanta totaled $800, but the extra three days increased the total bill to $1,200. You can deduct the $800, but not the additional $400.

• The extra days you spend in a city in order to take advantage of reduced airplane ticket prices count as business days, even if you use the extra days to sightsee.

These deductions only apply to the actual business person, and not to the spouse. Starting in 1994, most people can no longer deduct the expenses of a spouse who goes along on a business trip. The only exception to this rule occurs if both spouses are employed by the same company and have separate business reasons for traveling.

One way around this IRS ruling, is to drive to your destination. If you go by car, your spouse can ride along and you can still deduct $.29 per mile plus tolls, or actual expenses like insurance, gas, and maintenance. Full rental car costs are deductible, as is the full cost of a double room at a hotel.

If you travel outside the U.S., you have to meet one of four standards before you can make deductions for your trip. They are:

· You had no real control over the trip's arrangements.
This means you aren't management or related to the company, but you are simply seeking reimbursement for your travel costs.

· Your trip outside the U.S. lasts for seven days or less.
If you go to Algeria for a three day business trip and spend two days watching camel races, you can deduct expenses.

· The amount of time you spend on business during your foreign trip is at least 75 percent.
On a 20 day business trip, you spend 16 days seeing to your business and the other four days seeing the sights. The trip's expenses are deductible.

· Personal activities were not a major consideration when planning the trip. All you can do is document your expenses and activities and hope you can convince the IRS.

Conventions scheduled outside the U.S. are not deductible unless a legitimate reason exists for moving the convention outside the country.

Cruise trips are very difficult to deduct, especially since legitimate business convention expenses are capped at $2,000. In order to deduct the full $2,000 you need to be on a ship that is registered in the U.S. and only makes U.S. ports of call. You need to make a written statement concerning the number of hours spent every day in meetings, and you need to get a statement from the meeting's sponsor.

The most important thing to remember is to enjoy your travels. If some of these money-saving tips help increase your enjoyment because you are saving money, you might find the trip even more relaxing and fun.

THE FAST WAY TO SELL YOUR HOUSE

When you decide to sell your home, you don't want to be stuck for months waiting for a buyer. This is especially true if you depend on the money from your old home for a down payment on the home of your dreams. If housing markets are slow in your community, you might even feel like giving up selling your home because you think it will never sell anyway.

However, you are not trapped in your old home if you use a few common sense tips recommended by realtors across the country. The important thing is to make your house seem more appealing to a potential buyer than Joe's house down the road. Here is how you do it:

• Photographs

Take some photographs of the more appealing parts of your house, like a swimming pool, fireplace, or a tree-lined driveway, and a picture of the outside of your house. Attach all of these photos to copies of the floor plan of your house. As potential buyers take a tour, give an illustrated floor plan to them to take home. After a hard day of searching, all houses start to look the same in the tired brain of a buyer. However, your house will stand out because the buyer has photos and all the information at his fingertips.

• Change real estate agents

If a realtor has tried to sell you house for quite a while and no prospective buyer seems in the offing, change real estate agents. Sometimes a new agent has fresh views and ideas on how to sell your house. At the very least, the new agent might already have a buyer who is looking for a home like yours.

• Offer a bonus to your realtor

Tell the realtor that you will pay an extra $1,000 if he or she manages to sell your house within 30 days. If you depend on money from the sale of your house for a new down payment, the $1,000 is money well spent.

• Give buyers an incentive

Offer to pay half the points on the closing costs. This amounts to three to six percent of the purchase price, depending on your taxes, but it might be all you need to swing a buyer in your favor.

• Take your house off the market

If your house has been on the market for a few months without a sale, people begin to wonder what's wrong with it. Take your house off the market for a few months, and then relist it. Your house will seem like new property.

• Update the photo of your house

If snow appears in your real estate listing photo, and it's the middle of summer, buyers will know your house has been on the market for quite awhile.

It always helps to spruce up your property before you sell it. Put on a new coat of paint here and there, or plant a few more flowers. Don't forget, however, to also pay attention to the way your house is presented to the buyer—the more unique your presentation, the more your potential buyer will remember you.

FANTASTIC WAYS TO MAKE YOUR DOLLAR STRETCH

In a day and age when the national economy may not be doing so well and a person needs to watch every cent in order to get ahead, it's always a good idea to find new and creative ways to make your dollar stretch just a bit farther. Here are some unique ways to get the most out of your money while still enjoying your quality of life.

GAS

One way to save money on gas is to use your Discover Card to pay for all gas purchases. The Discover Card allows you to deduct one cent or more per gallon off the cash price at the pump. Even if you already own an oil company credit card, the Discover Card is still the better deal, because many oil companies charge a fee even when you use their card to buy gas. You can save even more money by paying off your Discover balance every month before the interest rates kick in.

SOFTWARE

Believe it or not, the U.S. Government spends at least $10 billion dollars a year on the development of new software for its different departments. What may be even more surprising is the fact that the government really doesn't keep a close track of what happens to all of this software.

Now, there is a way for you to try some of this top-of-the-line software for free. Gregory Aharonian compiles an annual report on 10,000 programs available from the federal government. Around 90 percent of these programs work on a personal computer, and reuse is usually not restricted.

The programs range from NASA's Control of Spinning Spacecraft software to financial, operational, and expert-systems programs designed for the IRS and the Commerce Department.

You can get Aharonian's report for $156.50 by calling Source Translation and Optimization at 617-489-3727. The report is available either on computer disk or on paper.

WEDDING DRESSES

Do you have a wedding with all the trimmings coming up in your near future? If so, consider renting a wedding dress instead of buying one. You can save hundreds of dollars and wear a beautiful designer gown down the aisle. Bridal apparel rental stores rent gowns which usually cost around $3,000 for as low as $400.

Be prepared to spend $100 to $200 up front, though, since most rental places require a deposit. The rental stores have the gowns professionally cleaned after each use.

JEWELRY

One of the best ways to save money on fine jewelry is to buy direct from the manufacturer. By doing this, you save yourself the extra costs of salesmen and jewelry store overhead.

George Thompson Direct offers its customers everything from solitaire and anniversary rings to diamond pendants, tennis bracelets, and diamond and precious stone settings. In a recent sale, a one-half caret diamond solitaire ring cost $599. The same quality ring in the national market cost approximately $2,600. George Thompson Direct offers deals like this by buying diamonds and gems around the world and then having the jewelry made in the United States.

For George Thompson Direct call 800-577-0005.

FREE AIRLINE PASSES

If you are in no great hurry to reach your destination, you can earn a free round-trip pass from airlines. The trick is to volunteer for an airlines "bump list."

As a rule, airlines regularly overbook their flights on the assumption that not everyone will show up for the flight. If too many people are scheduled to fly a particular plane, the airline will bump some of its passengers to the next flight out. This happens especially during peak times, like holidays and during summer.

The benefits of being bumped include an all-expenses-paid delay, a ticket for the next flight out, and a free round trip pass to one of the airline's destinations, usually in the United States, Mexico, or the Carribean.

FURNITURE

Who wouldn't love the joy of buying fine furniture and room accesories without the hassle of marching from furniture showroom to furniture showroom? Now there is a way to shop for furniture from the comfort of your own living room. By buying direct from one of the following catalogs, you can save a lot of time and money.

• Designer's Secrets, Box 529, Fremont, NE 27264, 800-955-2559. For a $2 catalog (refundable with the first $100 purchase), you can obtain furniture, drapes, bedspreads, and bathroom accesories.

• North Carolina Furniture Sales, P.O. Box 2802, Hickory, NC 28603, 800-248-6237. This furniture company offers more than 100 brands of furniture and in-home delivery. Order their free brochure for more details.

• Arthur M. Welling, 117 Old Rutherford Road, Taylor, SC 29687, 803-877-0852.   This company offers discounts on fine wood furniture. Their catalog costs $6.

• Ellenburg's Furniture, P.O. Box 5638, Statesville, NC 28687, 800-841-1420. Ellenburg's Furniture is an outlet for major furniture brands. The catalog is $6.

• Cherry Hill Furniture; Box 7405; Furnitureland Station, C1; High Point, NC 27264, 800-328-0933 or 800-888-0933.   Cherry Hill Furniture offers discounts on 500 major brands of home furniture, decorator items, rugs, and carpets. They can send you a free brochure or give you a price quote, and they deliver around the nation.

PET FOOD

Check out pet stores for free samples of food for each of your pets. Grab a handful of samples as you pay for your regular purchases, such as rawhide bones or catnip. If you visit two or three pet stores in a day and collect samples at each one, you can save a significant portion on your pet food bill. Look in particular for stores like Petstuff, which offer reduced rates on name-brand food and give away a lot of samples.

A CALENDAR OF MONEY-SAVING EVENTS

You might have noticed that certain items go on sale at certain times of the year, like Christmas cards do the day after the holiday. By paying attention to seasonal sales, you can save a great deal of money on both large and small purchases. The following list of seasonal sales may help you plan your future spending.

• January. This is the traditional time for after-holiday bargains. Pay attention to men's suits, linens in the mid-January white sales, appliances, and furniture.

• February. A lot of people might get married in June, but the traditional wedding gifts go on sale in February. Look for big price cuts on china, silver, glassware, bedding, and mattresses.

• March. Ski equipment goes on sale every March, and special pre-season spring clothing sales can snag a bargain.

• April. Items, especially clothing, come back on sale after the Easter holiday.

• May. By May, spring is definitely in the air all over the country, and with it comes spring cleaning. Watch for specials on household cleaning products, carpets, and rugs.

• June. Look around for good furniture buys, because the semi-annual inventory is arriving and all old items have to go.

• July. If you can wait until now to replace your summer products, do so. Stores liquidate their summer stock to make room for fall merchandise, so expect good bargains in garden tools and supplies, sporting equipment, and sportswear.

• August. August continues the sales on outdoor stuff, like lawn mowers, yard tools, patio furniture, barbeques and camping equipment. Also, car dealers mark down their current models to make room for next year's new merchandise.

• September. If you can convince your child to wait, buy the new school clothes at the end of September, when the hot new styles traditionally go on sale.

• October.   Do your Christmas shopping now instead of in December.   Stores offer bargains to boost retail sales before the long holiday season.

• November.   Wool clothing, especially men's suits and women's clothing, greatly decreases in cost this month as stores prepare for their second shipment of the season.

• December.   If you didn't buy your new car in August, now is the time as car dealers move out last year's stock before the end of the fiscal year.

When you plan carefully, shop around, and put off major purchases until they are at the lowest prices possible, you can save enough money to make your efforts more than worthwhile.   After all, it is your money and you should get the most out of it.

Last Minute Ways You Can Save Money on Your Taxes

You might be staring April 15 in the face, but there are still ways for you to lower the amount of taxes you have to pay. In order to do this, set up an individual retirement fund (IRA) or contribute to your existing fund, and deduct every possible thing you are allowed to deduct by the IRS.

INDIVIDUAL RETIREMENT ACCOUNTS

IRAs are wonderful inventions, because they not only give you an annual tax break when you need it, but they also allow you to receive tax-deferred interest on a fund you will need someday.

The best way to contribute to your IRA is in one lump $2,000 sum in January, instead of spreading your payments out over a 12-month period. By contributing the entire amount at once, you take full advantage of the money's ability to earn interest. At the end of the year, in an account earning nine-percent interest, you will have a total of $2,180, rather than the $2,100 you'd get with 12 months of payments.

In order to decrease your taxes, you can contribute to your IRA up until April 15.   There are some qualifications, however, which you must meet before your IRA contribution is considered tax deductible. They are:

• The money contributed to an IRA must be earned income—the money you make from salary, self-employment income, tips, or commissions. You cannot contribute money received from interest, dividends, rent income, Social Security, or a pension distribution.

• The amount you contribute is limited to $2,000 if you are single or if you and your spouse maintain separate IRAs, or $2,250 if your spouse does not work.

• If you are a part of a company-sponsored tax break, like a profit sharing or pension plan, you can't deduct your IRA contribution unless your adjusted gross income is less than $25,000 for a single person, or $40,000 for couples.

 Part of your contribution is deductible if you are single and your adjusted gross income falls between $25,000 and $35,000, or if your married adjusted gross income is between $40,000 and $50,000.

OTHER DEDUCTIONS AVAILABLE

• Although you cannot deduct interest paid on credit cards, you can deduct investment interest. The exception to this is if you borrow from your credit cards to buy stocks or other investments. The interest on your credit cards is then fully deductible against any investment income.

• Any charitable contributions, such as clothes, furniture, or money, is deductible if it is well recorded.

• Miscellaneous deductions are great, if you meet the criteria. You need to have more than two percent of your adjusted gross income in miscellaneous deductions before they count against your tax. Also, you can take the standard deduction or miscellaneous deductions—but not both. Miscellaneous deductions can include:
√ Some of your travel and lodging costs while you look for employment.

√ Safe-deposit box fees.
√ Investment counselor fees and investment service costs.
√ Union dues and assessments.
√ Any fees paid to a tax advisor to prepare your return or represent you during an audit.
√ The cost of small tools, safety equipment, and other job supplies.

• Any penalty you received from cashing in a certificate of deposit (CD) early is tax deductible.

• If you are the sole proprietor of a business or rental property, use a Schedule C (business) or Schedule E (rental property) to deduct the tax preparer's fee, instead of Schedule A. With Schedule A, you need to meet the two percent miscellaneous deductions' floor before it counts.

The very best way to take advantage of all deductions is to keep good records. Make sure you can find the information and proof when you need them. It also doesn't hurt to put away as much money as possible into tax-deferred retirement plans against the inevitability of next year's taxes.

RECOVER YOUR UNCLAIMED MONEY!

Whether you realize it or not, you may have a rightful claim to some of the more than $5 billion in assets which lies around in state offices across the country waiting for the owners to show up.

How is this possible? Well, sometimes people open accounts or rent safety deposit boxes and then forget about them. Often, when someone dies, not all the assets are accounted for in the will, so no one immediately claims them. Besides bank accounts and safety deposit boxes, the assets left unclaimed can include insurance claims, traveler's checks, dividend checks, money orders, and phone-line or other security deposits.

According to state laws, after five years holders of unclaimed property, such as banks, brokerage companies, insurance companies, and mutual funds have to make a reasonable effort to try and find the rightful owner. Usually, they try to contact the owner through the first class mail at the last known address. If their search fails, the assets are turned over to the individual state's abandoned-property division. The states then try to find a claimant by posting notices in the paper and by putting public service announcements on television and radio.

HOW TO CLAIM YOUR PROPERTY

If you think you might have a right to unclaimed property, there are certain steps you can take to retrieve it. They are:

1) Make a list of all former mailing addresses and residences where you or your deceased relative lived in the past.

2) Send this list of addresses along with your name and Social Security number, and the Social Security number of the person whose property you're claiming to the appropriate state's unclaimed property division.

3) While you wait for a reply, check any public listings of unclaimed property you can find. The locations of these listings vary from state to state, but most states print lists of unclaimed property in local papers. California's property lists are located on microfiche and a data base, as well as the more traditional sources. A list of addresses for all states' unclaimed property divisions follows.

4) If you establish that a state is indeed holding property which belongs to you, the next step is to properly prove your rights to it. The conditions for proving your case again vary from state to state, but many of them ask you to provide at least two forms of identification, such as a valid driver's license, a Social Security card, or a notarized birth certificate. You will also probably be asked to complete a claim form.

5) The final step is to wait for your assets to arrive. The return time varies, but most states respond with your property in three to six weeks.

UNCLAIMED PROPERTY AS A BUSINESS

Believe it or not, you can make money tracking down and reclaiming lost property on behalf of other people. Although state offices of unclaimed property exist to find rightful owners free of charge, many work on tight budgets and reduced staffs. The truth is, much unclaimed property never gets returned to people. About all most states do when searching for owners is print names in local papers a few times a year.

As a finder of lost property, you take over where the states leave off. In return for a flat rate or a share of the property, sometimes as much as 10 percent, you do the research and foot work required to identify, verify, and collect unclaimed assets for your customers. With $5 billion dollars in property unclaimed, you shouldn't be at a loss for clients.

A cardinal rule for being a finder is you need to know the state laws. First of all, check your own state laws and investigatory services to see if there is a cap on the amount a finder can charge a client for finding property. California actually issues separate checks to the claimant and the finder.

Secondly, many states only release money to the actual claimant, so it pays to know what individual state laws say. Send inquiries to each state office and ask for a copy of the state laws on unclaimed property, state laws dealing with finders, a description of the investigatory services available, and a number of claimant forms.

OLD STOCKS

If some of your unclaimed property turns out to be old stocks, don't just chuck them into the fireplace! Some old and seemingly worthless stocks are actually worth a lot of money.

Old stocks can be worth a great deal of money in two ways:
• If the company who issued the stock exists today in another form, you could find yourself owning shares in a major corporation. For example, your own stock issued in the 1970s for a tiny electronics company. After some research, you discover that electronics company merged with IBM in 1979. You suddenly discover IBM owes you some money.

• Even if your stocks are not worth anything today on the market, they could still have value as collector's items. Many collectors will pay big money for stocks signed by prominent people, like Henry Ford or John D. Rockefeller, or if the stocks have unusual artwork.

For more information on old stocks, check out The Directory of Obsolete Securities, published by Financial Information, Inc. of Jersey City, NJ; or Manual of Valuable and Worthless Securities by Robert D. Fisher. For a flat $50 fee, you can also have your stocks appraised by R. Smythe & Co.; 26 Broadway, Suite 271; New York, NY 10004.

LIST OF STATE UNCLAIMED PROPERTY OFFICES

Alabama
Unclaimed Property Division
P.O. Box 327580
Montgomery, AL 36132-7580

Alaska
Department of Revenue
Unclaimed Property
111 W. 8th, Rm. 106
Juneau, AK 99801

Arizona
Department of Revenue
Unclaimed Property
1600 W. Munroe
Phoenix, AZ 85007

Arkansas
Auditor of State
Unclaimed Property Division
230 State Capitol
Little Rock, AR 72201

California
Unclaimed Property Division
P.O. Box 942850
Sacramento, CA 94250-5873

Colorado
Unclaimed Property Division
1560 Broadway, #630
Denver, CO 80202

Connecticut
Office of the Treasurer
Unclaimed Property Division
55 Elm St.
Hartford, CT 06106

Delaware
Unclaimed Property Division
P.O. Box 8931
Wilmington, DE 19899

District of Columbia
Unclaimed Property Division
300 Indiana, NW, Rm. 5008
Washington, D.C. 20001

Florida
Abandoned Property Section
State Capitol
Tallahassee, FL 32399-0350

Georgia
Unclaimed Property Section
270 Washington St., #405
Atlanta, GA 30334

Hawaii
Unclaimed Property Section
P.O. Box 150
Honolulu, HI 96810

Idaho
Unclaimed Property Division
P.O. Box 36
Boise, ID 83722-2240

Illinois
Unclaimed Property Division
 Dept. of Financial Inst.
500 Iles Park Pl.
Springfield, IL 62718

Indiana
Unclaimed Property Division
219 State House
Indianapolis, IN 46204-2794

Iowa
Treasurer of State Unclaimed
Property Division
Hoover Bldg.
Des Moines, IA 50319

Kansas
Unclaimed Property Division
900 Jackson, #201
Topeka, KS 66612-1235

Kentucky
Abandoned Property Unit
Revenue Cabinet, Sta. 62
Frankfort, KY 40620

Louisiana
Unclaimed Property Section
P.O. Box 91010
Baton Rouge, LA 70821-9010

Maine
Treasury Department
Abandoned Property Division
State Office Bldg., Sta. 39
Augusta, ME 04333

Maryland
Unclaimed Property Section
301 W. Preston St.
Baltimore, MD 21201-2385

Massachusetts
Abandoned Property Division
1 Ashburton Pl., 12th Fl.
Boston, Ma 02108

Michigan
Department of Treasury
Escheats Division
Lansing, MI 48922

Minnesota
Minnesota Commerce Dept.
Unclaimed Property Section
133 E. 7th St.
St. Paul, MN 55101

Mississippi
Unclaimed Property Division
P.O. Box 138
Jackson, MS 39205

Missouri
Unclaimed Property Section
P.O. Box 1272
Jefferson City, MO 65102

Montana
Dept. of Revenue
Abandoned Property Section
Mitchell Building
Helena, MT 59620

Nebraska
Unclaimed Property Division
P.O. Box 94788
Lincoln, NE 68509

Nevada
Unclaimed Property Division
State Mail Room
Las Vegas, NV 89158

New Hampshire
Treasury Department
Abandoned Property Division
25 Capitol St., Rm. 121
Concord, NH 03301

New Jersey
Department of Treasurer
Property Administration
CN 214
Trenton, NJ 08646

New Mexico
Unclaimed Property Unit
P.O. Box 630
Santa Fe, NM 87504

New York
Office of Unclaimed Funds
9th Fl.,
Alfred E. Smith Bldg.
Albany, NY 12236

North Carolina
Escheat/Unclaimed Property
325 N. Salisbury St.
Raleigh, NC 27603-1388

North Dakota
State Land Department
Unclaimed Property Division
P.O. Box 5523
Bismarck, ND 58502-5523

Ohio
Unclaimed Funds Division
77 South High St.
Columbus, OH 43266-0545

Oklahoma
Oklahoma Tax Commission
Unclaimed Property Section
2501 Lincoln Blvd.
Oklahoma City, OK 73194-0010

Oregon
Division of State Lands
Unclaimed Property Sec
775 Summer St., NE
Salem, OR 97310-1337

Pennsylvania
Abandoned/Unclaimed Property
2850 Turnpike Industrial Dr.
Middletown, PA 17057

Rhode Island
Unclaimed Property Division
P.O. Box 1435
Providence, RI 02901

South Carolina
South Carolina Tax Commission
Unclaimed Property Section
P.O. Box 125
Columbia, SC 29214

South Dakota
Unclaimed Property Division
500 E. Capitol
Pierre, SD 57501

Tennessee
Unclaimed Property Division
11th Fl.,
Andrew Jackson Blg.
Nashville, TN 37243-0242

Texas
Texas Treasury Department
Unclaimed Property Division
Box 12019
Austin, TX 78711-2019

Utah
State Treasurer's Office
Unclaimed Property Division
341 S. Main, 5th Floor
Salt Lake City, UT 84111

Vermont
State Treasurer's Office
Abandoned Property Division
133 State Street
Montpelier, VT 05633-6200

Virginia
Department of Treasury
Division of Unclaimed Property
P.O. Box 3-R
Richmond, VA 23207

Washington
Dept. of Revenue
Unclaimed Property Section
P.O. Box 448
Olympia, WA 98507

West Virginia
State Treasurer's Office
Unclaimed Property Division
Capitol Complex
Charleston, WV 25305

Wisconsin
State Treasurer's Office
Unclaimed Property Division
P.O. Box 2114
Madison, WI 53701

Wyoming
Wyoming State Treasurer
Escheat Section
State Capitol
Cheyenne, WY 82002

Ontario, Canada
Office of Public Trustee
145 Queen Street West
Toronto, Ontario M5H 2N8

Everyone dreams of a phone call announcing that they are the long lost heir of Great-Uncle Waldo Wifflebrain, and these dreams may not be far from the truth! Although it does take some time, searching through a state's unclaimed property division can be worth your while, especially if you in any way suspect that some property in your family hasn't ever been accounted for. Some letters, research time, perhaps a few phone calls, and you, too, could get your share of the $5 billion in lost property!

WOULD YOU LIKE TO WIN THE LOTTERY?

This is a silly question, of course. Everyone at some point in their lives dreams of winning the lottery and plans how to spend every cent of it. Your answer to the above question might be: "Certainly, I would love to win! But I haven't got a chance of winning a really big jackpot."

Would it interest you to know there are ways of winning the big jackpots? Although it doesn't change you overall odds, by playing certain unpopular combinations of numbers, you can greatly increase the amount you can win. In a typical state-run lottery where you are asked to pick six numbers between 1 and 49, there are about 14 million different combinations available. Of these, approximately 20 percent, or 2.8 million are not chosen by anyone in an average game. The trick is to pick numbers which fall within the unchosen 20 percent. Here are the numbers to target:

• Choose numbers which are over 31. Most people feel they have a foolproof system when they play combinations of birthday and anniversary dates. This leaves many numbers over 31 unclaimed. Actually, four of your six choices should be 32 or greater.

• Pick numbers which end in 0, 1, 2, 8, and 9. Most people choose numbers ending in 3 through 7. In fact, almost nobody uses 10, 20, 30, and 40.

The most popular numbers—and the ones to avoid—are:

• Single digit numbers. Do not use more than one number which falls within the 1 through 9 range as part of your six choices.

• Multiples of 7. Lucky 7 strikes again, and for the superstitious, it's the only way to go.

• Numbers which form horizontal, vertical, or diagonal patterns on your bet slip card. Many people like the idea of shouting "BINGO!" when they win the jackpot.

• The combination 1-2-3-4-5-6. Avoid this like the plague, because it is probably the most popular combination.

By playing the unpopular numbers, you stand a good chance of being the only winner of a jackpot. In fact, you can increase the amount of prize money you get by up to 600 percent!

HOW TO LOWER THE COSTS ON YOUR DREAM VEHICLE

If you are like most other people, you carry a picture of your dream vehicle in your mind. Perhaps your vehicle is a Mercedes Benz, a BMW, a Porsche, or even an eight-cylinder Dodge Ram pickup truck.

Whatever your ideal vehicle looks like, several ways exist for you to realize your dream without it costing you a fortune. Among your choices is using a car buying service to find the best price, taking a trip to Europe to buy a car, or leasing a vehicle for less than it would cost to buy it. If your dream vehicle is a potentially classic model, you are in an even better position to own it once you learn the classic car ropes.

CAR BUYING SERVICES

For a nominal fee, car buying services can take the work and worry out of finding that good bargain on a new car out of your hands. Because they solicit bids on new cars from at least five area dealers, they can often cut as much as $3,000 to $10,000 off the sticker price.

Several car buying services even handle all the paper work, so the only thing you have to worry about is finding a ride to the dealer to pick up your new car. Here is a list of reliable car buying services you might like to contact:

• Automobile Consumer Services, (800-223-4882). The fee for their service is $295, but they may deliver the car to your door.

• Autoadvisor, (800-326-1976). Their car buying service costs $249.

• Carbargains, (800-475-7283). For $135, Carbargains arranges the bid, and you finalize the deal.

• Consumers Automotive, (703-631-5161). Depending on the car's price, the fees for this service range from $195 to $395, but they do everything, including deliver the car to your driveway.

NEW CAR TAX BREAK

You can take as much as $1,000 off the total state and local taxes you need to pay on your new car. Ask the dealer to subtract the trade-in value of your old vehicle before he calculates the taxes on your new car.

This option is not available in Alaska, California, Maryland, Michigan, Virginia, or Washington, D.C.

BUY EUROPEAN IN EUROPE

If your dream vehicle is a European import, consider traveling to the source to pick it up. Purchasing a European car in Europe can more than save you enough money to cover the cost of your trip, especially if currency rates are in your favor.

For example, a BMW 750IL typically costs $80,900 in the U.S. If you bought the car in Germany, it would cost you $71,200. A Mercedes 300E (3.2 liter) costs $49,900 in the U.S. The same car in Europe goes for $44,550.

In order to take advantage of this, you need to remember the vehicle you buy needs to be built for sale in the United States. If your lovely new car has a steering wheel on the right side, you are out of luck. Talk with your local car dealer for more information.

EXTENDED CAR WARRANTIES

Any time you go into a dealer in search of a new vehicle, one question that inevitably comes up is whether or not you want to purchase an extended warranty. The answer you give should depend on whether you intend to keep the vehicle for a few years or trade it off next fall.

If you plan on keeping your car, an extended warranty is an excellent idea. Most of today's cars are loaded with electronics and technology, and there is nothing unusual in some part of your sophisticated vehicle breaking down after 30,000 miles.

Most factory-backed extended warranties are negotiable, so don't accept the first $800 or $1,200 warranty price offered to you. Instead, say you'll pay half the asking price, and don't agree to any more than two-thirds the initial warranty cost. Whatever you do, make sure the warranty you buy is backed by the factory.

CAR LEASING

If you would prefer not pouring lots of money into car payments, perhaps leasing a car is for you. You can get a tremendous bargain on a vehicle by leasing instead of buying.

For example, the average car today costs around $21,000. After you've made a 10 percent downpayment and four years of monthly payments, that car now cost you $26,000. After leasing the same car for four years, you probably put $16,000 into the deal altogether. So you end up $10,000 ahead in the long run by leasing.

Another item which might make leasing pay off is the consideration of whether your $26,000 car will be worth $10,000 in four years. If it won't be, you probably come out ahead by leasing. The $10,000 you save can be applied toward two or three more years of lease payments on another car.

If you can manage it, the cheapest way to lease a car is to pay the entire amount of the lease at the beginning. Say you want to lease a $30,000 car. Lease payments over a three year period will cost you $14,000, but you can save $2,000 by offering a one-time $12,000 payment.

The greatest disadvantage to leasing is the car still belongs to someone else. Whatever money you put into the car is gone forever and you won't be able to get any of your funds back by reselling the vehicle.

COLLECTIBLE CARS

Sometimes it can really pay to concentrate on restoring a collectible vehicle, especially if it's a car you really want anyway. When you hear the word "collectible," you probably think of Ford Model As or the straight eights of the 1930s, but a collectible car can be any model whose value will increase with time. Even within models manufactured within the last 20 years, certain cars deserve to be called classic.

When you don't have thousands of dollars to spend on a pre-1960 model car, the next best thing is to pick up a collectible car manufactured in the last 10 years and hang on to it until its value increases. Sometimes an initial investment of $10,000 to $20,000 can give you a piece of property worth $20,000 to $40,000 in 10 years!

• Recent collectible cars.
The cars which people will want to pay lots of money for in 10 years tend to be high performance models and convertibles. Cars worth investing in include:

√ 1994 Mustang Mach 3 ("The Viper Killer")—This supercharged, 4.6 liter beauty is sold on a limited edition basis.

√ 1980s Mustangs—Currently, they cost from $10,000 to $15,000, but in 10 years they might be worth $25,000 to $35,000.

√ 1960s Mustangs—These Mustangs cost $12,000 to $20,000 now, but they will probably appreciate to $25,000 to $45,000 in th next 10 years.

√ Late 1970s and 1980s Corvettes—Right now, they cost $30,000 to $50,000, but in 10 years, they'll be worth $50,000 to $100,000.

√ ZR1 Corvettes—These cost $70,000 to $100,000 now, but may be worth as much as $250,000 in the next century.

√ Lincoln Mark 8—Currently, it costs $35,000 to $40,000, but it is outselling and outperforming all other luxury performance cars.

√ 1994 Camaro Z28—This vehicle matches the Corvette for body and high performance.

√ Also check out 1971-72 Barracudas, 1970-72 Chevelles, all other Corvettes, the Datsun 240Z, and the Datsun 260Z.

• Collectible car values.
Like other collectibles, such as stamps or money, the better the condition of your car, the more money it will be worth on the market. Professional classic car dealers rate vehicles on a scale of one to five:

√ Number 1—This is a museum quality car with very low miles and totally, authentically restored. On a scale of 1-100, it rates a 95.

√ Number 2—The number two car is also low-mileage and fully restored, but there are a couple of things not quite right about it. For example, the car might be a 1966 model, with a 1968 grill. It gets an 85-95 rating.

√ Number 3—These cars aren't in perfect condition, but they've been well-restored and have low mileage. Most of the cars displayed at car shows are number three cars. They get a rating of 75-85.

√ Number 4—This is what you see before someone does restoration work, and number four cars need total restoration.

√ Number 5—It is beyond the physical capacity of man to restore a number five car. All it is good for is parts.

In order to protect yourself from paying number one prices for a number three car, have an appraiser do a thorough check of the car to see how much it is worth. Appraisers charge either by the hour or by a percentage of the car's total worth. To avoid an excessive bill, try to locate a "by-the-hour" appraiser.

• Where to find collectible cars

Probably one of the best places to look for a reasonable collectible car is the want-ads of newspapers. Often, owners let collectibles go at bargain prices, either because they don't want the car anymore or they just don't realize how valuable their property is.

You can also find collectible cars at car auctions, car shows, auto trader magazines, and through auto appraisers. One company which specializes in auctioning collector cars is Kruse International. They auction off more than 12,000 collectible cars of every make, model, and era every year. For more information, contact: Kruse International, P.O. Box 190, Auburn, IN 46706 (219-925-5600).

HOW TO CONTEST A WILL

Nothing can cause more anger or hard feelings within a family than the reading of a will after someone's death. In a sense, people find out for the first time how a deceased person really felt about them. If the estate is large, and someone feels cheated or left out, they will probably get a lawyer and contest the will.

This is what happened to the estate of the late J. Seward Johnson, heir to the Johnson & Johnson fortune, after his will was read. Johnson left his entire $400 million fortune to his young chambermaid, whom he had just recently married. His children, who were independently wealthy, were left completely out of the will. They sued.

After four years and about $15 million in legal fees, J. Seward Johnson's estate settled with his children. They received $100 million of the estate, whether their father wished it or not.

Contesting a will creates more than simple family strife—it is time-consuming and puts a financial burden upon your heirs to defend the property they inherited from you. How can you prevent this from happening?

As you make out your will, consider the following facts and suggestions. In most cases, you can guard your will from a contest, if you know how.

· **Leaving children out of your will**

Although your children will disagree with you, nowhere in the Ten Commandments does it say, "Thou shalt leave thy Porsche to thy son and thy summer cottage to thy daughter."

In other words, if you feel strongly about it, you aren't required by law to leave anything to your children. But your heirs should be prepared for a fight, especially if your estate is large. The ways to protect your will from a contest by your children are:

√ Mention them in your will

When you mention them, you prove that you did not accidentally overlook their existence. Usually, if parents want their children out of the will, they will mention them and will them a dollar.

When you do not mention children in a will, they can contest on the grounds that it was an accidental oversight on your part and you really did mean to leave them something.

√ Put your money into a living trust

With a living trust, you transfer your assets into a trust while you are still alive. Then, by naming yourself trustee, you can retain control over your estate. When you die, a successor trustee takes over.

Your assets avoid the probate court, so your children have no way to contest your will. They might try, but it would end up costing a great deal of money, and chances of succeeding are very slim.

· **Disinheriting a spouse**

Legally, you cannot leave your spouse out of your will unless he or she agrees to it. No matter how terrible your relationship, in most states your spouse is automatically allowed one-third of the estate. In the states of Arizona, California, Idaho, Louisiana, Nevada, New Mexico, Texas, Washington, and Wisconsin, you spouse's entitlement rises to 50 percent of the total estate.

This situation is known as "forced share." Literally, the spouse forces the estate to give a portion whether it's agreed to in the will or not. The only way to avoid a forced share situation is to have the spouse sign away his or her rights to forced share in return for a fixed portion of the estate. Even then, spouses occasionally contest the will in court if they feel they didn't receive enough.

· · **Ex-spouses**

Once your divorce is final, you are no longer responsible for the financial health of your ex-spouse. Unless you feel obliged to, you do not have to leave any portion of your estate to your ex.

· The criteria for contesting a will

Will contests are not the exclusive privilege of spouses and children. Anyone who feel he would benefit if all or part of the will is found invalid can contest in court.   The contestants can be grandchildren, distant relatives, or friends.

Occasionally, wills are overthrown in court, usually because the contestants could prove one of three things:

√ The will was not properly signed

Make sure you sign and date your will just as you would any other legal document. And find at least two reliable witnesses to sign with you.

√ The person who made the will was not mentally competent at the time of signing

This one is very difficult to prove, because eccentricities do not necessarily prove mental incompetence.   A man can leave his entire fortune to his springer spaniel and three Japanese goldfish if he wants to.

√ The person was induced to sign through fraud or "undue influence."
Sometimes people are tricked into signing a new will. Someone they trust makes them think all they are signing is some paperwork for joining a new health spa, when in reality they just signed a new will. This constitutes fraud, and it will not hold up in court.

Undue influence occurs when someone convinces or threatens you into signing a will in favor of the threatening person. For example, what if your grandparents became convinced that a local charlatan was really the prophet of God, who required every cent of their estate to keep the wrath of God from falling on their heads. You and your relatives can prove undue influence in court and have the "prophet's" will overturned.

Any will is subject to a contest, even wills dealing with smaller estates. However, the thing to remember is that contesting any will can be a very expensive proposition. A typical contest can cost the people involved $25,000 or more just in legal fees. This is because most estate-litigation lawyers ask for a large retainer fee, reimbursement on any costs incurred, and possibly a portion of the settlement.

Another fact the contestant should consider is that 99 percent of the contested wills which go to court are not settled in favor of the contestant. On top of this, in some states if the court rules a contestant's claim has no basis, he ends up having to pay for all legal fees on both sides.

One final way you can take care of any potential contestants to your will is to write an anti-contest provision into your will. This simply tells your heirs that any one of them who contests the will in search of a bigger portion automatically loses whatever he inherited.

Of course, this means willing people enough of the inheritance to make contesting a dumb idea. But sometimes anti-contest provisions are worth the peace it can buy for your heirs.

MINIMIZE TAXES WITH THESE ESTATE PLANNING TIPS

If you worry about how much Uncle Sam will take from your estate in taxes after you die, you are not alone. Of all your "heirs," Uncle Sam is by far the most demanding. He expects to be paid up front, and unless you plan in advance, he will take a large portion of your estate for taxes, leaving your relatives and friends with a lot less than you—and they—bargained for.

There are several ways to minimize estate taxes, and you should consider each one before you finalize your last will and testament. A very important part of planning you estate is to get the most out of the $600,000 estate tax exemptions allowed by law.

Technically, the first $600,000 willed by each individual or couple is estate tax free. However, if you and your spouse have more than $600,000 in property, you lose the opportunity to leave your heirs up to $1.2 million in estate tax free property as long as you claim to be a couple when setting up your estate.

The secret is to separate the assets of a married couple so that the couple becomes two separate individuals where estate taxes are concerned. Here is one way to accomplish this.

REVOCABLE LIVING TRUST

One method available to a couple is the revocable living trust (RLT). When you set up a RLT, all the property you put into it exists as a separate entity from you, in very much the same way as a corporation. However, you don't have to worry about losing control of your assets. In an RLT, you remain in control of everything. You decide who sets up the trust and who benefits from it—and you can act as both beneficiary and trustee. You also decide who acts as trustee and who benefits upon your death.

One key to making the RLT work is to make absolutely sure that you legally retitle all your assets into the name of the trust. If you do not make the trust the legal owner, the RLT loses its effectiveness, and all the work that went into setting it up becomes a waste of time. Retitling can be done through a $25 do-it-yourself kit, or through a trust company for a fee of about $1,000. If you decide to set the RLT up yourself, make sure you get an attorney who is familiar with trusts review your paperwork.

Another reason to use an RLT is to avoid having your property go to probate court upon your death. This decreases the chances of someone contesting your will and tying your property up in court for a long period of time.

How does the RLT work to the advantage of a married couple? When a couple has more than $600,000 in assets, the RLT allows them to divide up their estate into two parts to take the most advantage of the estate tax free clause. This process creates what is known as an "A/B trust" or a "His and Her trust."

Part A to setting up an A/B trust is to take exactly $600,000 of cash or property which is tax exempt and either:

• Give this portion directly to your on the death of the first spouse, with the remainder of the estate going toward the maintenance of the surviving spouse.

• Or you can put the first $600,000 into an RLT, giving your children title to the assets, with the provision that they cannot touch the money while the remaining spouse is still living. The surviving spouse then receives income from the trust until death.

Part B of the A/B trust covers all assets left after the first $600,000. Whether the remaining amount is $50 or $5 million, all of it goes to the surviving spouse without having any estate tax slapped on it. This is because of the marital by-pass rule which allows a surviving spouse to inherit any amount of money estate tax free.

Normally, the marital by-pass rule simply means that the government defers taxes on a couple's estate until the death of both spouses. Then the government collects estate taxes on the combined remaining assets of the couple before any heirs can claim property.

The beauty of the A/B trust is $600,000 of your property is already estate tax free because of your RLT. Because you split up your estate into two portions, The government can only get estate tax money from the part B portion of your estate. However, $600,000 of this part B portion is also estate tax free, thanks to your spouse's individual $600,000 exemption.

Legally, you can leave your heirs a large estate while saving them at least $120,000 in estate taxes!

LIFE ESTATE

If you are a retired adult, you've probably heard the same piece of advice over and over—give your house to your children while you are still alive so that Medicaid doesn't seize the property later to pay for nursing homes and medical care.

Most of the time parents want their children to inherit all of their assets. There is a big tax problem, however, with simply signing a home over to the children. If you were to sign your house over to your children at this point, Uncle Sam would set their cost basis at what you originally paid for the house, not at what the house is worth at the time you sign it over.

Let's use an example to explain this further. Say you originally bought your house for $50,000, and it is now worth $150,000. When you children sell the house at some point down the road, they will end up paying major taxes on any money they receive over $50,000. If they sell the house for $250,000, they will have to pay taxes on $200,000!

The way to get around this taxing problem is to set up a life estate, especially if your assets total less than $600,000. With a life estate, you can gift your home to your children, give them a big tax break after you die, and still live in the house for the rest of your life. The life estate sets up a lifetime tenancy which expires at your death.

Thirty months after the date you set up your life estate, the value of your home becomes your children's asset, not yours. So, if you ever need to enter the nursing home, Medicaid can no longer lay claim to your home.

After you die, your children's cost basis is stepped-up to the date when you die, not left at the home's value when you bought it. In other words, if your home is still worth $150,000 when you die, and your children manage to sell it for $200,000, they only pay taxes on $50,000 instead of the original $200,000.

Upon your death, the life estate affects your heirs' taxes in two ways:

• The value of the home at your death will be included as part of your entire estate for estate tax purposes.

• If your house is worth $150,000 when you gift it over to your children, that amount immediately reduces your lifetime gift exclusion of $600,000 down to $450,000. This is something to keep in mind if you are in the habit of giving your children annual $10,000 checks (any annual gift under $10,000 is free of gift taxes). If you've already given your children $500,000 in gifts, they are going to end up having to pay taxes on at least $50,000. So pay attention to the total amounts you've given as gifts over the lifetimes of your children.

OTHER ESTATE PLANNING TIPS

Here are some other items you should know before you finalize your estate plans.

• Joint title is not a great estate planning idea.
Although joint tenancy can help you avoid probate court, it has some major disadvantages. If the holders of the joint tenancy are someone other than a spouse, a portion of the property will be included in the estate of the first to die, based on the amount of money that person contributed when the property was bought. This means the property is subject to estate taxes.

Also the co-owner loses the benefit of the step-up in the tax basis discussed above. If you have joint ownership with someone and you inherit the whole property upon his death, you could face substantial taxes when you sell that property.

If you hold all your property jointly with your spouse, you lose the advantage of that additional $600,000 amount that is estate tax free.

• Putting up to $10,000 per year in a trust for a child does not guarantee you avoid the gift tax on the money.
In order for the $10,000 to be a gift, your child needs to be able to get to the money and spend it. By putting the money into a normal trust, it becomes a permanent part of the trust. That means your child cannot get to the money right away.

The accepted way around this problem is to make sure the trust you set up for your child has a "Crummey clause" which allows the child to withdraw the gift within 30 days. If the child does not withdraw the money in this time period, the gift becomes a permanent part of the trust. Make sure the trustee informs your child with a written notice every time you use the Crummey clause in relation to a gift.

• You don't necessarily escape the gift tax if you give each of your children $10,000 every December 31

Two things can happen here which can ruin your chances of avoiding the gift tax in this situation.

First of all, you have to consider any other monetary gifts you might have given your children throughout the year. A one or two thousand dollars here and there might not seem like a lot to you, but if the IRS notices these gifts, it will add them all up and charge a gift tax on any amount over $10,000.

The other problem arises because of the fact the IRS believes a gift is not a gift until the check clears the bank. If you give your children the gifts on December 31, 1994, and they do not cash the checks until after January 4, 1995, you have already met the $10,000 gift tax free limit for 1995. If you forget and give your children more $10,000 gifts on November 30, 1995, someone ends up paying large gift taxes on these extra $10,000 gifts.

• It may not be entirely wise to leave all your property to your spouse.
If you have property worth more than $600,000 and leave everything to your spouse, you are giving up the opportunity to take advantage of the extra estate tax free $600,000.

• If you own your life insurance policy, it is included in the total amount of your estate.
When you pay the premiums on your life insurance policy, or you are able to borrow against the policy or cash it in, you are considered the owner of that policy. Since you are the policy owner, the cash value of the insurance policy will be added to your estate upon your death. This means your beneficiary might have to pay estate taxes on it.

The way to avoid this problem is to let someone else own the policy, like your spouse or a child. The policy owner should be the one who pays the premiums, although you can make gifts to the policy owner which can be used to pay the premiums. Whatever you do, avoid the trap of owning the policy or paying the premiums directly if you want your beneficiary to avoid paying extra taxes.

• Holding onto property just because gift taxes are too high is not necessarily a good idea
There are three items you should remember here. First, the tax tables for gift and estate taxes are identical. Secondly, the amount of gift or estate tax your beneficiaries need to pay depends on the value of the property. Finally, most property appreciates over time.

You can do your heirs a big favor by giving them gifts now, rather than a large chunk of property later. Giving them the gifts now allows them to pay gift taxes on property at its present value instead of having to pay estate taxes on property which may be worth a lot more at a future date.

If you would still prefer to leave your heirs a single chunk of property instead of giving them gifts, try to get rid of any appreciating property if possible. Of course, if you need the property to maintain your lifestyle, by all means keep it.

But if you have appreciating property which is just lying around because you don't really need the money, you should sell it so your heirs are not stuck with the extra taxes for property which has greatly increased in value.

• If you decide to leave your assets directly to your grandchildren instead of to your children, make sure the amount of the inheritance falls within the $1 million per grandchild bracket.
Money left to grandchildren instead of to children is subject to the "generation-skipping tax." Designed to discourage the leaving of assets directly to grandchildren, this tax is a double estate tax of any amount of money over $1 million that you might leave to your grandchildren.

You can avoid the generation-skipping tax by making sure you leave no more than $1 million to each grandchild. Give any remaining assets to you children and ask them to buy life insurance or do whatever else is necessary to avoid extra estate taxes.

By planning now, you can make the transition of your assets to your beneficiaries as smooth and simple as possible. Besides, you worked hard to save your money and collect property. Wouldn't it be better to use these legal methods to insure that the people you love receive as much of your estate as possible upon your death? If you don't make arrangements now, Uncle Sam will be looking for more than his fair cut later.

HOW TO AVOID EXPENSIVE LEGAL FEES

Let's face it—there are times in everyone's life when you need a good lawyer. In some circumstances, however, you can have your legal needs met by an experienced nonlawyer. Nonlawyers do not cost nearly as much as regular lawyers, and sometimes they can cut through the red tape faster, saving you a great deal of money.

For example, when it comes to filling out the forms in an uncontested divorce suit, a lawyer may charge the client around $1,200 for the service. An experienced nonlawyer can probably fill out the same papers for $300.

The routine real estate closing is another situation where a nonlawyer can come in handy. Lawyers usually charge about $100 to handle a routine real estate closing, while a nonlawyer will do the work for a fraction of the price. (Check your state's laws on real estate closings, because some states require a lawyer's presence.) Other legal areas where a nonlawyer can be used include:

• Arbitration
Frank S. of Wilmington recently got into a dispute with the securities company which did some investing for him in certain high priced securities. Something went wrong with the deal, and Frank lost most of his invested money. He decided to take the securities company to court on the ground that they were unduly careless with the investment of his money. The dispute between Frank and the company goes into arbitration, where a neutral party can settle the disagreement.

Frank has three choices. He can represent himself, but this can be risky because he stands less of a chance in prevailing in the arbitration case. Frank can hire a securities lawyer, who knows the ins and outs of arbitration. This will cost him at least $5,000 up front, plus expenses, plus one-third of any award he wins. Frank's third choice is to find a nonlawyer who is an arbitration specialist. The cost of the arbitration nonlawyer is a less than $5,000 upfront fee and 20 percent of any award. Frank goes with the nonlawyer, wins the arbitration, and the whole legal business ends up costing him a lot less than if he had hired a securities lawyer.

• Mediation

Mediation is much kinder, gentler, and less expensive than arbitration. Since any decision made is non-binding, a dispute settled through mediation often takes a lot less time and hard feelings to finalize. If you want to stay in the goodwill of the party with whom you are disputing, try mediation first.

In mediation, the pre-trial exchange of papers is done away with, and the mediators move back and forth between the opposing parties. Sometimes it takes as little as an hour to have a dispute mediated to a successful conclusion.

When searching for a nonlawyer, ask for references and check him out before you trust your legal business to him. Like any other profession, there are good, competent nonlawyers and then there are frauds. Know what you are getting into before you use one.

THE DO-IT-YOURSELF WILL

Many people can make their own will without the bother and expense of lawyer or nonlawyer fees. You might have seen do-it-yourself will kits advertised in different places for $12.95.

Now, for one dollar to cover postage and handling, you can get a free will kit from an organization known as LegalEase. If you are interested, write to: LegalEase, #C183, 1801 miller Drive, Lynchburg, VA 24501.

INSURANCE TIPS, OR "KNOW WHICH WAY THE BALL BOUNCES"

Buying and collecting from insurance companies can be a frustrating, confusing, and sometimes frightening event, if you don't know what you are doing. Like any other business, insurance companies exist to make money, and many companies will do anything they can to make sure they keep their money. Their methods might range from overcharging you for premiums, to underinsuring you, to cancelling your policy after you file a claim.

What can the average insurance customer do? The answer to that question is PLENTY. Your most important weapons are your brain and your telephone. Use your telephone to shop around for good reliable insurance bargains (even the major companies have ways in which you can save money).

Once you have information on several policies, use your brain to read the policies thoroughly to make sure you know exactly what you are getting before you sign anything or send a check to anyone. When it comes to information, it's okay to use an insurance agent, but remember that insurance agents usually get a commission from a company for selling you an insurance policy. The agent might not have your best interests in mind. Your best bet is to go directly to the individual insurance companies for information, and then deal with an agent once you've decided what you want.

If you want the best coverage for your money, it is up to you to stay informed on the best ways to save on premiums, to know what your insurance will and won't cover, and to understand what to do if your insurance refuses to pay your claim. Here are some tips on buying and collecting from insurance companies.

SAVE MONEY ON YOUR PREMIUMS

The best ways to save money on your premiums is to dig through your policies at regular intervals and make sure they are up to date, ask for discounts if they apply to you, know what your policies cover, and shop around for the best deals.

• Auto insurance.
There are several methods you can use to save money on your auto insurance premiums. They are:

√ Talk to different companies before buying insurance.
Remember that not all insurance companies are alike, and that you might pay different prices for the same coverage. Talk to different companies and see what they offer. If two companies will give you the same coverage, but one company's premiums cost twice as much as the other, your shopping around tactics will have paid off.

√ Ask for discounts.

Many insurance companies have discounts on premiums if you are classified as a low risk driver. Call your insurance agent and see if you apply for any of the following discounts. The percentages in the parentheses are the typical savings you would get on the entire premium, unless otherwise noted.

* Female, age 30 to 64 (25%).
* Senior citizen (5% to 15%).
* Farmer (10% to 30%).
* Good student (25%).
* Student away at school (10% to 15%).
* Anti-theft alarms (5% to 15% on comprehensive coverage).
* Passive restraints (10% to 30% on the no-fault or medical part of the premium).
* Car pool for getting to and from work (15% to 20%).

√ Raise your deductible on comprehensive coverage.

When you pay a low deductible, you are filing small claims, which raises premiums in the long run. Consider instead changing your deductible to between $500 and $1,000. You can save as much as 30 percent on the premium for all comprehensive coverage except collision damage.

√ See if some of your insurance needs are covered under other policies.

If you have medical insurance already, and your auto policy also covers injuries to yourself and your family, it isn't worth paying twice for the same coverage. Drop that part of your auto insurance.

√ If your car is old, don't bother with collision insurance.

You pay for collision insurance based on the cost of your car when you bought it, not on what it is presently worth. If your 10-year-old car gets totaled in an accident, your insurance company will probably pay you a few hundred dollars for its actual market value at the time of the accident.

This means that all the hundreds of dollars you've spent over the last 10 years for collision insurance went right into the insurer's pocket. The best way to handle this is find out the blue book value of your present vehicle and decide if its value is worth all the extra expense of collision insurance.

√ Be a good defensive driver.
Just by being a good driver, you can decrease the amount you spend on auto insurance premiums. This means watching out for the other drivers, wearing a seatbelt, and SLOWING DOWN.

By doing all these things, you reduce the risk of having accidents which require filing claims to your insurance company. Also, if your driving record shows that you've had several moving violations or other "points," your premium might be as much as 10 percent higher than if you had no violations.

• Homeowner's insurance.
With your homeowner's insurance, see if you can arrange to insure your home for 80 percent of its value instead of for the whole 100 percent. This is based on the idea that, no matter what happens, there is usually something salvageable in your home. Almost no house is a total loss.

By getting 80 percent coverage, you can save as much as 10 percent on your premiums. Shop around for the best policy, however, because some insurance companies will penalize you for getting the 80 percent coverage by paying the cash value on your loss rather than replacement costs.

• Life insurance.
The three most popular forms of life insurance are term insurance, credit life insurance, and insurance which is also an investment. Before you choose your insurance, remember the reason why you want life insurance—you are trying to protect your family from hardship in case you die.

√ Term life insurance.
If you need to buy life insurance, term life has the best bang for the buck. It is pure insurance, and the least expensive life insurance available. The average premiums for term run about 70 percent less than you would pay under an insurance-investment policy.

In order to make the most of your term insurance, buy annually renewable term insurance and switch companies every five years. This tactic takes advantage of the fact that most insurance companies offer deals to new subscribers for the first five years of the policy.

√ Credit life insurance.
You usually see credit life insurance when you sign a loan for a big ticket item, like a car. It is sold through banks, auto dealers, and other lenders, and simply makes sure that the lender gets all his money back on the loan even if you die.

It may sound logical and affordable, but it can end up costing you more than it is worth. When you agree to buy credit life insurance, you end up paying money to insure the loan principal, the insurance premiums, and all financial charges. In other words, you are taking all future risk upon yourself. It's a great deal for the lender—you pay all the money to have him insured!

√ Insurance-investment policies
Insurance-investment policies can also cost you more money than they are worth. Because of heavy commissions and fees which come from the fact that you are buying both insurance and an investment, a portion of your premium gets eaten up in the costs every month instead of being put to work earning interest for you.

Another problem which can arise in an insurance-investment policy is that your money may not be entirely safe. It may not be wise to invest money in the insurance industry considering that some companies are unstable and may go bankrupt.

Plan ahead before you decide to drop your insurance-investment policy. When you drop a whole life or universal life policy, you are subject to taxes on the earnings you've received on the principal (the principal is not subject to these taxes). If your earnings add up to a lot of money, roll them over into a tax-free annuity, with the same company if possible. Then buy a term life insurance policy.

· Low cost term insurance by phone
If you want to locate good term insurance without leaving the comfort of your home, there are a variety of businesses which specialize in finding the right term insurance for less money.

√ Selectquote (800-343-1985) helps consumers locate low cost policies with highly rated companies. The service is free to callers, because Selectquote gets a commission from the company whose policy is selected.

√ Insurance Information, Inc. (800-472-5800). This group charges a $50 fee for its services, unless it fails to save you at least $50 compared to what you now pay for your present policy.

√ Insurance Quote Services (800-972-1104). Insurance Quote Services gets a commission, so the service does not cost you anything. It sends updates four times a year on low-cost term policies to all its clients.

• Long-term care policies
Long-term care insurance policies are designed for older people who want additional protection against the high costs of nursing homes or home medical care. The nice thing about these policies is that you can take the policy offered by the insurance company, or you can design your own policy to fit your needs and to save money. If you decide to design your own long-term care policy, here are some guidelines you should follow:

√ Put together a daily benefit amount that's lower than the average daily cost of nursing home care in your area.
By doing this, you can save as much as $300 in premiums every year. For example, you discover that nursing homes in your area cost an average of $150 per day. Make your policy out so that the insurance company pays $125 a day, and you pick up the extra $25 per day with your own funds.

√ Choose a four- to six-year cumulative benefit period instead of accepting lifetime benefits.
This move can save up to $1,000 a year in premium costs.

√ Write in inflation protection.
You want your long-term care policy to be worth something when you need it. By adding an inflation protection clause, you automatically increase your initial benefit level at least five percent every year to keep up with inflation.

If you decide to go with an insurance company's ready-made policy, many companies offer long-term care policies. There are enough differences between policies to enable you to find the one which is best for your situation. Listed below are three companies which offer long-term care policies, a description of these policies, and the costs of premiums.

√ UNUM (tel. 207-770-2211).
UNUM's policy includes a $100 per day nursing home benefit, a $50 per day home care benefit, a 90-day elimination period, a six-year benefit, and a five percent compounded inflation clause.

√ CNA (tel. 312-822-5000).
This insurance company offers a $125 per day nursing home benefit, a $50 per day home care benefit, a 90-day elimination period, a four-year benefit, and a five percent compounded inflation clause.

√ AMEX (tel. 415-492-7000).
AMEX offers a $125 per day nursing home benefit, a $50 per day home care benefit, a 100-day elimination period, a four-year benefit, and a five percent compounded inflation clause.

Annual Premiums for Each Company:

AGE:	60	65	70
UNUM	$1,600	$1,363	$1,400
CNA	$2,233	$1,643	$2,258
AMEX	$3,024	$2,357	$3,240

Take your time making your decision about which long-term care policy you want to go with. Be sure the one you choose is the best one for you.

• A Freebie

Do you want to learn more about health insurance? If so, write to the Health Insurance Association of America and ask for The Consumer's Guide to Health Insurance. This manual explains what kinds of health insurance policies are available, what the differences are between group and individual insurance, and contains a glossary of common insurance terms.

For your free copy, write to: Health Insurance Association of America, Box 41455, Washington, D.C. 20018.

KNOW WHAT YOUR INSURANCE COVERS

Once you buy insurance, it is easy to assume that all your worries are over. As long as you pay your monthly premiums, your insurance will protect you from any bad incidents.

That is not at all the case, however. In many instances, insurance does not cover everything automatically. It is extremely important to read your insurance policy thoroughly and know what is and is not covered under the policy. Once you know the facts, you can work to find additional coverage, and you won't get a nasty surprise after something happens.

Here are some items which you need to look into further to make sure you have adequate coverage.

• Liability

Your homeowners policy usually covers a certain amount of liability if, for instance, someone slips on your icy step or your dog bites the mailman. Your insurance company picks up the costs of your legal defense, along with any damages you might have to pay.

The problem with liability occurs when the damage settlement is for a greater amount than the limit set by your policy. If your policy has a $100,000 limit and your mailman sues for, and receives, a $500,000 settlement, you could be in big trouble.

One way around this situation is to buy an umbrella liability policy. This kind of a policy can protect you against large future liability settlements.   A normal $1 million umbrella policy will cost you around $100 to $250 a year.

• Medicare

If you think Medicare automatically picks up all medical expenses you might have, you are wrong.   Medicare has many ways of getting out of paying for many items.

For example, you end up paying a $676 deductible for hospital stays, and you are responsible for a large part of the bill for any hospital stay that exceeds 60 days. If you need a surgeon, an anesthesiologist, and an ambulance, your costs include a $100 deductible and at least 20 percent of the bill for these services.

You can protect yourself against these additional charges by obtaining Medigap insurance. Like the name implies, Medigap literally plugs any holes in your present Medicare coverage and protects you against a lot of extra expenses.

• Foreign travel

Before you leave the United States, make sure you know whether your health insurance covers the cost of accidents and hospitalization in foreign lands. It probably does, but it is good to know in case something happens.

What should you do if you find yourself laid up with a broken leg in a Swiss hospital? The first thing you should do is contact your insurer. Make sure you carry your insurer's phone number. When the Swiss hospital won't accept your insurance card, but will accept your credit card to pay for your hospital bill, all you can do is pay with plastic and send an itemized bill to your insurance company once you get home.

One thing you need to know is that Medicare usually doesn't cover medical expenses outside the United States. If your Medigap or other insurance also refuses to cover you, consider buying travel medical coverage. The rates are about $50 per person for a two week trip to Europe.

• Safety deposit boxes

Most people don't realize that the contents of their safety deposit boxes are not covered by the bank. If the bank is robbed or burns to the ground and you lose all your possessions, it is not the bank's responsibility to reimburse you. Also, your normal homeowners insurance policy usually covers the contents of a safety deposit box only to around a $500 limit.

Your alternative is to add a rider to your homeowners policy which specifically protects your deposit box. The cost of this kind of protection is usually about six dollars for every $1,000 coverage. If you only use your box to store your stock and bond certificates, additional insurance isn't necessary since new copies of these certificates can be reissued if stolen or lost.

However, if your safety deposit box also contains your most prized valuables, additional insurance is a must. Before you buy additional insurance, make an inventory of everything you keep in the box, along with an appraised estimate of what everything is worth. This list might include stock and bond serial numbers, important personal papers, contracts jewelry, silverware, or home ownership records.

When you have valuable items like jewelry or silverware, bring in a professional appraiser to assign a proper value to your belongings. You don't want to shortchange yourself by underestimating the value of your property. After your inventory is finished, keep a copy separate from the safety deposit box and update it periodically.

POTENTIAL PROBLEMS YOU MIGHT HAVE WITH YOUR INSURER

When it comes to money, insurance companies are just like any other business—they love to see the money pour in, but they don't like spending money. Whenever possible, many insurance companies try several methods to avoid paying settlements on claims.

A good working rule for you is that the higher the claim, the more likely it is that you will have a fight getting everything owed to you. However, if you know some of the basic tricks insurance companies use to avoid settlements, you can be on the lookout for them and they won't come as such a shock. The methods used include:

• Failure to completely investigate claims
Almost every state has laws which say it is the insurer's duty to investigate policyholders' claims in good faith. This means the insurance company should look at all the evidence and pay up accordingly.
What happens sometimes is the insurance company denies the claim until they contact the appropriate experts, such as

doctors, contractors, or appraisers, or they might contact the experts in order to find a reason not to pay.

If your claim is unfairly denied, your first step is to go to your insurance agent and submit statements from experts who can support your claim. When the claim includes damage to property, photos or videotape can also help you establish your claim. If your insurer still refuses to accept your claim despite all the evidence, find a good trial lawyer.

• Unwarranted rescission
Unwarranted rescission means your insurance company tries to cancel your policy after you file a claim. This can happen in any form of insurance, but it is most common where health insurance is concerned.

What happens is that insurance companies normally do not investigate your application until after you file a claim. When you file a claim, they hire an adjuster whose sole job is to audit your medical records to see if you left something off of your application.

If they can find anything at all which they can tie into your present claim, they will try to cancel your policy to avoid paying a settlement. For example, if you file a claim for broken leg treatment, and the adjuster discovers you failed to mention your bout with pneumonia on your application, the company may connect the two somehow and cancel the policy.

The laws which cover this subject are rather clear. If you didn't know you had the medical problem at the time of your application, or if you failed to recognize the significance of your omission, or if the omission has nothing to do with your medical problem, the insurance company cannot cancel your policy.

The best way to avoid this problem is to answer all questions on the application as honestly as you can. Do not depend on your agent to fill out your application, but rather do it yourself, since agents tend to paraphrase questions in ways which might get you in trouble someday.

For example, the agent might ask you if you have any problems with your blood pressure when the actual question asks if you have ever been treated for high blood pressure.

• Overturned medical opinions
Whenever insurers review a claim, they ask the question, "Was this treatment really necessary?" Often, in order to determine the answer to this question, insurance companies bring in "in-house" medical examiners, or hire "independent" medical examiners who might be influenced by the fact that the insurer pays their salary.

Many times, these medical examiners decide that the policyholders' doctors were wrong in their opinions and the treatment was in reality unnecessary. The result is thousands of unjustly denied claims every year.

You have two choices here. Most health policies willingly pay for a second opinion, so get an additional doctor's opinion on record. Also, use doctors who are willing to fight for your rights, if necessary.

• Denying health claims which received preapproval
Every year, many policyholders follow their insurer's instructions and call for preapproval before receiving treatment. Therefore, it is a great shock when the insurance company denies the claim on the grounds that the treatment was unnecessary, experimental, or excessive.

What happens in these cases is the policyholder talks to a clerk who verifies the policy is active and the treatment is covered by the company. The key is that this does not mean the insurer approves the idea of you receiving the treatment. Clerks cannot give preapproval. The only insurance company staff members who can do this are claims adjusters.

When you call the company for preapproval, make sure you talk with a claims adjuster. If your claim is still denied, because the treatment was "experimental," ask your doctor to contact the insurance company and explain why you were a good candidate for the treatment. If the insurance company still refuses to settle your claim, contact a good attorney.

• The usage of low-priced contractors
Auto and home insurers often base their settlements on estimates obtained from contractors who do inferior work for low rates. Before you get your car or home fixed by the insurer's contractor, check around and get other estimates from independent contractors.

Evaluate the discrepancies between the independent contractors and the insurer's contractor. If you are not pleased with the insurer's contractor, negotiate with the company for a different settlement. Most insurance companies are willing to compromise.

• Refusal to pay full-replacement value on home contents
When customers go off in search of homeowners insurance, many of them are careful to buy policies which promise to pay replacement costs, rather than market value. This can be a wise move, since it can cost far more to rebuild a home than the market value is worth.

One problem you can run into with this strategy is that full-replacement coverage often comes with a capped amount which is far less than it would take to rebuild your home. Another problem is that policies are often unclear on whether the coverage extends to your belongings as well as the home itself. Finally, the insurer may demand receipts for everything on which you file a claim—something most people cannot provide.

In order to combat these problems, read your policy thoroughly to make sure the caps on your full-replacement coverage are not too low. Check also to see what the status of your belongings is in the policy. Make an inventory of all the belongings in your home. Keep a copy of the inventory in your safety deposit box and give a copy to your insurance agent.

Insurance can be a great item to have, because when you buy insurance, you buy peace of mind. In order to get the most out of your insurance, however, you need to stay on top of what your policies are doing and what you can do to increase the value of your policies.

One thing to remember is that no matter how good insurance can be, you do not want to end up "insurance poor." This means that you spend so much money on insurance policies for you car, health, and home in an attempt to protect yourself against every potential problem—tornado, typhoon, flood, fire, accident, and theft—you end up with hardly enough money on which to live comfortably.

If you recognize yourself in the above description, relax and accept the fact that it is impossible to insure against every little thing which might happen to you. Carry the insurance policies which are most important to your situation, and get rid of the rest which guarantee insurance against remote possibilities. After all, who needs typhoon insurance in Nebraska?

HOW TO WITHDRAW YOUR IRA MONEY BEFORE RETIREMENT

How often have you heard people say that you can't take money out of your individual retirement account (IRA) before age 59-1/2? Common knowledge says you can't touch your IRA before you're 59-1/2 without paying taxes and a stiff 10 percent penalty. But this just is not true. A way exists for you to take full advantage of your IRA money long before you are ready to retire, with out paying the penalty (you are still responsible for any taxes on the withdrawn money).

One thing to remember—IRAs should not be looked upon as being another bank account. You should only withdraw money from them before retirement age for special reasons. They are:

• You take a leave of absence or stop working for a period of time and you need extra income.

• You decide to go back to school and you need cash to further your education. Or you need the money to help pay for your child's education.

• You are laid off unexpectedly, or you are involved in a medical emergency.

• You need the money to start a promising small business.

If you fit into any of the above categories, and you decide to remove money from your IRA, the first step is to contact the person or company that manages your IRA. Ask him to set up an amortized life expectancy annuity with your IRA. This means that your IRA will be distributed to you annually in equal payments for as long as you are expected to live.

The key is life expectancy. Using the IRS life expectancy tables, your IRA custodian will divide the amount of money in your IRA by your life expectancy and factor in an expected annual rate of return. If you want a copy of the IRS life expectancy table, call 800-TAX-FORM and ask for Publication 590, or see the chart below.

Life Expectancy Table

AGE	YEARS	AGE	YEARS
44	38.7	50	33.1
45	37.7	51	32.2
46	36.8	52	31.3
47	35.9	53	30.4
48	34.9	54	29.5
49	34.0	55	28.6

The beauty of an annuity is that your IRA continues to earn high interest even as you take money out. For example, if you are 50-years-old, your life expectancy is 33.1 years. You decide to set up an amortized life expectancy annuity with your $50,000 IRA, which earns 10 percent annual interest. You could take out $5,223 a year for the rest of your life expectancy with out hardly touching the IRA's $50,000 principal. This can be done because your money earns close to $5,000 in interest every year. Therefore, you are actually removing only $223 of the principal. At this rate, your $50,000 IRA will last a very long time.

AMORTIZED LIFE EXPECTANCY ANNUITY GUIDELINES
There are only two guidelines which you must follow in order to set up this kind of annuity.

• You have to take annuity distributions until you are at least 59-1/2-years-old and you need to receive the distributions for at least five consecutive years. In other words, if you start withdrawing at age

57, you must stick with the annuity until you are 62, which is two-and-one-half years after you can normally withdraw non-penalized IRA funds.

• Your annual annuity distributions must be roughly equal

For many people, there is no problem with this rule. But if you've already set up an amortized life expectancy annuity for $5,223, and you suddenly become very ill, you are stuck with the first annuity amount for at least five years—whether you need extra money or not.

An amortized life expectancy annuity is not for everyone, and those who decide to go with it should realize all the implications of what they are doing. In a sense, people who accept this kind of annuity are gambling with the future, because they need to work under the assumption that nothing will happen to change their future needs for IRA funds. And sometimes you have to take that risk, if you really need the extra money.

The best bet, though, is to leave your IRA untouched so it can continue to gather interest as long as possible.

WHERE TO COMPLAIN ABOUT PROFESSIONAL ADVISERS

What do you do when a professional adviser takes advantage of you? No matter how much you checked credentials and personal references, that lowdown skunk of a securities broker ran off with your life savings, or your insurance company simply refuses to pay for anything even after initially agreeing to do so, or perhaps the lovely home of your dreams that your local realtor assured you was in mint condition turns out to be a fire hazard and a rat trap.

Although the vast majority of professional advisers are exactly that—professional—some bad eggs do get mixed up in the lot. If you feel a professional adviser has wronged you and you want redress, it pays to know who to get in contact with. The following suggestions and addresses give you a starting point in your search for justice:

CONSUMER PROTECTION

Contact:

• Federal Trade Commission (FTC); Sixth Street and Pennsylvania Avenue, NW; Washington, D.C. 20580 (202-326-2180).
The FTC can handle complaints about mortgage bankers, retail stores, consumer finance companies, and other creditors. It also has a vested interest in the prevention of false advertising and telemarketing and investment fraud. Because it is an independent government agency, any consumer is free to contact the FTC with complaints about a faulty product or creditor.

LEGAL

• American Bar Association (312-988-5000).

Because lawyers are registered with the bar associations within the states where they practice law, your best bet is to contact your local state bar association. The state bar associations handle complaints about lawyers on a case-by-case basis. If you cannot get in touch with your local bar association, call the American Bar Association in Chicago at the above telephone number.

• Organization of Americans for Legal Reform (HALT); 1319 F Street, NW, #300; Washington, D.C. 20004, (202-347-9600).

HALT is a national non-partisan, non-profit organization whose goals are to help people handle their legal affairs simply, affordably and equitably. For a $15 annual fee, you receive a membership with HALT which entitles you to a free copy of "Using a Lawyer and What to Do When Things Go Wrong," as well as access to a legal information and referral network.

INSURANCE

• State Department of Insurance.

If you have a complaint about your insurance company, you should first contact your state department of insurance. This government entity keeps files on state-licensed insurance companies and agents.

However, not every insurance policy falls under the jurisdiction of state departments of insurance. If you run into trouble with one of those mail order policies you see on T.V. or you have a "certificate of insurance" through a group or organization, these plans do not usually fall into individual state regulations. When in trouble, you need to work through the insurance department of the state where the insurance company has its home office.

• National Insurance Consumer Helpline (800-942-4242).

This helpline is sponsored by the American Council of Life Insurance, the Health insurance Association of America, and the Insurance Information Institute—all of which are trade organizations which represent health, life, and property or casualty. They may not be able to help you with individual agents or insurance companies, but the can deal with problems in existing policies. When you call the helpline, these organizations will either intercede on your behalf or hand your problem over to the appropriate association.

• National Insurance Consumer Organization (NICO); 121 N. Payne Street; Alexandria, VA 22314, (703-549-8050).

NICO is a non-profit public interest organization whose primary interests are educating consumers on the wise purchase of insurance, helping states with insurance reforms, and monitoring the situation in the insurance industry as a whole. The annual $30 fee is tax-deductible.

REAL ESTATE

• State Real Estate Commission or Regulatory Agency

When you have problems with a real estate agent or broker, about the only place you can complain is to your state real estate commission or to the proper regulatory agency. All a state real estate commission can do is revoke a realtor's license, censor the realtor, or administer fines for violations like incompetency, theft of escrowed money, or misrepresentation of a piece of property.

If you lost money to a crooked realtor, the only opportunity you have to get your funds back is to take him to civil court.

SECURITIES

• Securities and Exchange Commission (SEC); 450 Fifth Street, NW; Washington, D.C. 20549. (Consumer Affairs Office: 202-272-7210)

The SEC regulates investment companies, investment advisers, transfer agents, and broker dealers. If you bought securities from any of these sources and feel wronged in some way, the SEC can investigate your claim.

• National Association of Securities Dealer (NASD); 1735 K Street, NW; Washington, D.C. 20006, (202-728-8000 or 800-289-9999).
NASD is every consumer's dream—a self-regulatory organization which works to maintain the integrity of the securities industry. Not only does it monitor brokerage firm compliance with federal securities laws, but it also works to solve complaints and problems investors might have with the securities industry. This is particularly important, because investors usually waive their right to sue brokers and brokerage houses when they open an account.

Among their services to investors, NASD arbitrates disputes between investors and brokers, and operates a free information line which anyone may call to find out the work and disciplinary histories of people who work in the securities industry.

Just because a person has a professional background, it does not mean that he is above the law and there is nothing you can do if you get taken advantage of. Contact the appropriate agency or organization and see what you can do to solve your complaint in your favor.

THE INS AND OUTS OF PUBLISHING YOUR BOOK

There is an old saying which states that everyone has one good book in them. If you have already written yours, or you have a good idea for a book, you are already halfway to your goal of being published. Now the trick is to attract the attention of a publishing house.

Like any other business, publishing companies exist to make money. You need to sell your manuscript to a publisher in such a way as to make him want to read it. Some books are available which can help you not only sell your idea, but also walks you through the process of publishing a manuscript, so the business doesn't make you feel overwhelmed.

The books are:

• The Insider's Guide to Book Editors, Publishers and Agents by Jeff Herman. Herman's book will take you step-by-step through the world of publishing. The first thing you do when using this book is to identify the companies and editors who specialize in your type of book. Next, write a query letter to the editor and explain in one page what your book is about, why you wrote it, and why he should publish it. You need to capture the editor's attention right away and make him say, "I want it!"

Always send your query to a particular editor, instead of to the publishing company, or your letter will get lost in the shuffle. Never send your manuscript without first sending a query letter. Most companies won't even look at an unsolicited manuscript.

• Another indispensible book for the writer is Writer's Market: Where and How to Sell What You Write , edited by Mark Kissling and Jenny Pfalzgraf. This book is the writer's bible. A new edition hits the book stores every September, so make sure you have the most up-to-date edition. Writer's Market lists not only book publishers, but also magazine publishers, playwright publishers and greeting card companies. It has a great deal of good information, and even carries interviews with published writers.

• Vanity or subsidy publishers—Unless you plan only on distributing a few copies of your masterpiece to friends and relatives, avoid vanity and subsidy publishers. They can cost a lot more money than they're worth.

• Poetry. If your inclinations lean toward poetry, there is a way for you to enjoy your talent and make money also. Some greeting card companies are constantly looking for fresh talent, and they are willing to pay a minimum of $5 per word. You can earn an extra $15,000 or more just by writing verse every night in front of your TV!

The way to take advantage of this is to buy some three- by five-inch index cards. Type your verse on one side and your name and address on the other. Sort your verses by subject, put them together with a a self-addressed stamped envelope, and send them to the card company of your choice. You will probably hear back from the company within 30 days. If they reject your poems, you can try sending them to other card companies.

Tip: Don't bother sending poems to the really big card companies like Hallmark and American—they use mostly in-house writers.

You can send your poems to:

Amberly Greeting Card Company, 11510 Goldwest Drive, Cincinnati, OH 45249. Amberly specializes in humorous cards.

Oatmeal Studios, Box 138, Rochester, VT 05767, if you have birthday or holiday poems.

Paramount Cards, Box 6546, Pawtucket, RI 02940. This company deals mainly in "you to me" poetry.

• You can obtain a free catalog of books for writers by writing to: Writer's Digest, 1507 Dana Ave., Cincinnati, OH 45207. Whether you are interested in novels, greeting cards, or television scripts, they have a book for you.

Writing can be such a relaxing hobby, but it is even more fun and exciting if you have publication as your ultimate goal! Why not give it a try? You could be the next Hemingway or Danielle Steele!

MONEY STRATEGIES FOR ALL PERIODS OF YOUR LIFE

No matter what your age, there are ways to earn extra money through savings and investments. The secret is to take command of your money and invest it in ways which are appropriate for your time in life. In order to be ready for retirement, you need to make long-term goals, and work to reach those goals.

Without careful planning, your retirement may end up a lot less than you expect, as you scramble and scrimp to stay on a tight budget at a time when you should be enjoying your leisure. Here are some pointers on earning extra money and saving that money so that you get the most for your buck when you need it.

WORK TO SAVE

The best way to save enough money for investment is to watch your spending closely. Divide a sheet of paper in half and make a list of all your expenditures on one side and all your income on the other. If your expenditures exceed your income, you probably will feel like you don't have any money left to save for a rainy day.

There are ways around cash flow problems, however.

• Set up your own home business that you can work at in your spare time. This might be something as simple as tutoring local students or as complicated as sewing wedding dresses—whatever you have the talent to accomplish. Some people have part-time businesses managing other people's household accounts.

The money you make from your second income can go directly into a savings and investment plan, and over time the amount can really add up without disturbing your normal lifestyle.

If you don't have the time for a second job and you own your home, consider renting out a room in your home. Depending on where you live, you can get around $300 extra per month. This extra money can go into a savings plan.

• Authorize automatic deductions from your paycheck for company pension or profit-sharing programs. If the company you work for doesn't have such a program, set up your own automatic savings plan by arranging with a no-load mutual fund to make monthly transfers from your checking account into a mutual fund account. If any raises or bonuses come your way, try adding that to your mutual fund.

You can put away up to $2,000 tax-deferred into an individual retirement account (IRA) every year. The important thing is by having the money deducted automatically, you don't spend the money if it's not in your account waiting to be spent.

• After you finish paying for a large item, like a car, an appliance, or student loans, continue to set aside money for payments. The money goes directly into your savings account. This means that if you paid a $300 a month car payment, and you continue to deduct the same amount from your budget, at the end of a 12-month period you will have $3,600 in savings.

Any spare cash can go into savings. Instead of buying that new stereo system with your income tax refund, save it. You will get a lot more use out of your money in the long run.

SAVINGS PLANS FOR THE STAGES OF LIFE

Having a savings plan in effect isn't just for middle-aged people anymore. These days, it can pay for a youngster to have a savings plan established, just as it can pay for a retired person to continue making certain investments. Investments can be made at any time of your life, but the secret is to take advantage of investments which which work best for your age at this time.

• Children

Technically, children can make up to $3,700 before they may have to pay any taxes. If the child sets up an IRA plan which allows him to invest $2,000 every year, he can increase his total non-taxable income to $5,700.

This IRA plan applies only to money the child earned and not to money received from interest and dividends. If your child decides this is a good idea, make sure the wages he receives are appropriate for the job he does, or the IRS may disallow those wages.

• 20s and 30s

√ Buy a home.

If you are somewhere in your 20s or 30s you are at the peak age to buy a home. This is because most residences carry a 30 year mortgage, and you can have your house paid for before you retire.

The best investment is a single family home, rather than a condominium. By buying now, you get a tax break and your housing costs come under control.

One item to avoid is the temptation of a home-equity loan to help pay for other debts, like credit card bills. Although the interest is less than you pay for your credit cards, this sort of loan can eventually endanger your ownership of your home.

This is because many of these loans are structured so that you pay interest only, with a large balloon payment of principal due at a later date. If you are in enough financial trouble to need a home-equity loan to pay off your debts, chances are excellent you won't have the money when the principal comes due.

√ Stocks.

Now is also the time to buy stocks if you want to make your money grow significantly. You should put 70 percent of your long-term investment money into stocks or stock mutual funds. The other 30 percent should go into bonds or bond funds.

If you have the option of investing your money into your company's stock, think about it carefully before you put all your money into one place. You could become overly dependent on the fortunes of your employer. If your company loses a great deal of money, you stand a chance of losing both your investments and your job.

√ CDs.

For more leeway, consider buying certificates of deposit (CDs) from a brokerage house instead of from a bank. It costs more initially, because the broker charges a fee and banks do not. However, often brokers can offer a higher interest rate which more than offsets the initial cost, and brokers usually allow you to sell a CD before its maturity date without any penalty.

If you are in your 20s and save 10 percent of your annual gross income, you can have a tidy amount available when you retire. If you are already in your 30s, you should try to save 15 percent of your annual income. If you plan to retire early, you need to save even more of your annual income—say 20 to 25 percent— in order to insure you have enough money available when retirement rolls around.

√ Insurance.

Obtain enough insurance to cover any potential incident. Many younger people feel they don't need insurance at their age, but an accident or illness can wipe out savings and opportunities to invest in the future. Among the insurances to look into, besides the standard health and life policies, are disability insurance and umbrella-liability insurance in case you are ever sued.

• 40s and 50s.

√ Portfolio.

By your 40s, your portfolio should consist of 50 to 60 percent stocks and the remainder should be in bonds. As you come within 10 years of your projected retirement age, change the types of securities you invest in so that you are more protected from potential failure. Move your money away from growth-mutual funds and more into growth-and-income funds. Also, work to buy higher-quality bond funds instead of high-yield junk bonds.

Try to invest as much money as possible into tax-deferred savings, like IRAs, variable annuities, and 401(k) plans. Without this strategy, you might end up paying a lot more tax than necessary.

√ Estimate your retirement income.

As you reach your 40s and early 50s, make a yearly estimate of how much retirement income you think you'll need to live comfortably. By doing this, you can see the potential weak spots in your savings plan and work to save even more, if necessary.

Now is also a great time to find out how much your Social Security payments will amount to. If you decide to retire at age 62, you are entitled to 80 percent of your benefits, or 47.5 percent of your spouse's benefits. Choose whichever amount is higher.

For a woman who was out of the work force a long time while raising a family, she might get more money by depending on her husband's Social Security than upon her own. Call Social Security at 800-772-1213 and get estimates for both you and your spouse before you make a final decision.

If your plan depends on receiving Social Security benefits before age 65 in order to cover retirement expenses, you don't have enough income in investments and should stay in the work force longer to build up your savings.

√ Pay your mortgage.

Work hard to get your mortgage paid of before retirement. Without the extra cost of mortgage, your cost of living will decrease dramatically and your money will stretch much farther.

If you cannot pay your mortgage off completely before retirement time, at least work to refinance your home if low interest rates are available. When you wait until you retire to finance, you might discover that banks don't want to refinance your mortgage because your income will be lower than when you were still working.

When refinancing, avoid adjustable-rate mortgages and do not extend to length of the loan. Obtain a fixed-rate loan with a shorter pay-back time instead. You want to lock in your low interest rate and pay off your home as soon as possible.

While you are at the bank refinancing, think about setting up a home-equity line of credit, because you will have trouble arranging this kind of credit line once you are retired. Use this home-equity line of credit for emergencies and to pay for high-interest credit card debts.

√ Insurance.

Another item to find out about if you plan to retire early is your health insurance. When you retire at 62, you have three years to go before Medicare begins to cover your medical bills. Find out whether or not your employer continues to provide your insurance after your retirement.

If not, get a Blue Cross/Blue Shield policy or check out your local health maintenance organizations. Try to avoid obtaining a policy from smaller or lower-rated insurance companies, because they might suddenly cancel your policy.

The 40s and 50s are also the ages to begin planning your estate. You should have three items as part of your estate plan—a will, a power of attorney or living will in case you can no longer make your own decisions, and a living will with a health care proxy.

• Retirees

You have reached the golden time of your life, the time when you can truly relax and enjoy yourself. But that doesn't mean you should let your money lay around getting flabby.

√ Portfolio

Continue to deal in the stock market. If you are in your 60s, put 40 percent of your investments in stocks. People age 70 or over should have at least 30 percent invested. Consider higher-quality securities, such as equity-income mutual funds.

Because stocks tend to have larger returns than bonds, concentrate your stock market investments in your IRA an other tax-sheltered accounts. Your bonds can go into your taxable accounts. Use the money from your taxable accounts first and let your IRA money continue to collect interest and enjoy its tax-sheltered status as long as possible.

Continue saving a certain part of your investment gains instead of spending it all. Reinvest money at least until you are 75. This insures that at least part of you money's value will not be decreased because of inflation.

Consider cancelling your life insurance policy. In many cases, there is no longer any reason to protect a non-working spouse from the death of the spouse who earns the money. You might need your premium payments to cover other debts.

√ Update your estate

Check your estate plans every so often and make any necessary adjustments. Sometimes you might have to change the beneficiaries of your will because of divorce or death in the family. Keep your family informed of the state of your health, finances, and health care arrangements.

Most important of all is you should discuss any major financial decisions with someone you trust. Scam artists work hardest to sucker retired people. One bad decision and you could find years of planning, hard work, and saving down the drain.

RETIRE TO A FOREIGN COUNTRY

If you do not have a great deal of money, but you would still like to enjoy an adventure upon retiring, then perhaps retirement to a foreign country is for you! Two countries worth considering for such a plan are Brazil and Mexico. Both of these countries have good food, friendly people, and low costs of living—if you know what you are doing.

• Brazil.

If you've ever dreamed of living somewhere with a warm climate, fun-loving people, and a cost of living which makes US$500 a comfortable retirement amount, then consider moving to Rio de Janeiro, Brazil.

With an average temperature during the coldest month of 71 degrees Fahrenheit, Rio de Janeiro can indeed be a nice place to live. It is located on the coast of the south Atlantic, and is known for its cosmopolitan attitudes and Mardi Gras celebrations.

Rio de Janeiro can be a fun city in which to live, as long as you avoid getting caught in the tourist traps. If you avoid the fancy restaurants, hotels, and stores, you can easily live off of a pension as small as US$500 to $1,000 a month.

This means, of course, that you will be eating the local foods, which is nutritious and tastes good. Also, you probably won't be living right on the water front, but you have a good chance of locating a 900-square-foot single bedroom apartment near the beach for as little as US$200 a month. The best hospitals in the city cost somewhat more than hospitals in the U.S., but you can buy Brazilian health insurance for about $100 per month.

How is all of this possible? The secret lies in the high level of Brazilian inflation. Brazilian inflation can easily go as high as 32 percent, and the governments current policies almost guarantee that inflation will continue high for several more years. Since the American levels of inflation are not tied to the Brazilian levels, your US$500 will be worth as much as 30 percent more every month. This is like receiving an extra $150 in purchasing power every month.

Prices are adjusted every six months to make up for inflation, but that means you are making money in the interim, and your rent is actually much less than $200 per month. Although you will probably have to be frugal for the first few months, your money will quickly build its purchasing power because of inflation. It won't be too long before you can live very comfortably, indeed!

For more information, contact the Consular Section of the American Consulate, Avenida Presidente Wilson 147, Rio de Janeiro 20030-020, Brazil (tel. 011-55-21-292-7117).

• Mexico.

Like Brazil, Mexico has the distinction of being one of the most affordable places in the world to retire to. All it takes to set up residency in Mexico is knowing your way around the red tape.

√ Foreign status

Foreigners in Mexico are divided into three groups—FMT, FM2, and FM3. If you are strictly a tourist, you receive the FMT status. This means your papers are good for 30, 60,90, or 180 days. Although some Americans duck the law by remaining in Mexico on FMT papers, they can only legally be issued once a year to the same person. If you are caught with expired FMT papers, you could be told to leave the country.

Foreigners who receive FM3 status can stay in Mexico for more than six months and up to five years. In order to be FM3, you must have an income of at least 3,700 pesos per month, or 1,800 pesos if you already own a house in Mexico. You also must have an additional 1,800 pesos per month for each of your dependents. With FM3 papers, you cannot work in Mexico or ship furniture into the country. You can apply for FM3 papers at the Mexican consulate.

If you want to retire to Mexico, your best bet is to apply for FM2 status, which makes you a permanent legal resident. As an FM2, you can bring one houseful of furniture into the country, although shipping costs can be very expensive. After five years, you may also work anywhere in the country.

In order to apply for FM2 status, you must be at least 55-years-old, and have an income of 5,900 pesos per month, or 2,950 pesos if you already own a Mexican home. You also need 2,950 pesos a month for each of your dependents. All FM2 applications must be approved in Mexico City.

√ Cost of living in Mexico.

Mexico is a very reasonable place to live. Groceries run about 56 pesos a month. If you ship in or buy furniture, an unfurnished apartment in the city can cost 466 pesos a month, and unfurnished homes go for 466 to 3,732 pesos a month.

A furnished room starts around 2,070 pesos a month, with an additional 10 percent a month tax added. With the utilities, the gas costs about 28 pesos per month; the electricity, 62 pesos per month; and the water, 62 pesos per year. You probably will have enough left over to hire a maid at about 105 pesos per week!

√ Contacts.
For more information about retiring to Mexico, contact:
* Mr. and Mrs. F.G. Fulton, Apdo. 5-409, 3A, Guadalajara, Jalisco, Mexico (tel. 52-3-621-2348 or 52-3- 647-9924). The Fultons publish a newsletter called Retiring in Guadalajara.

* Guadalajara/Chapala Update, MRTA, P.O. Box 2190-23, Henderson, NV 89009-7007, USA.

* Cuernavaca Calling, Dr. G.H. Gilbert, Apdo. 4-587, C.P. 62431, Cuernavaca, Morelos, Mexico.

* Mexican Meanderings, Southwind Information Service, P.O. Box 33057, Austin, TX 78764, USA.

It always pays to learn as much about a country as possible before you decide to spend the rest of your life there. If possible, take a trip or two to your chosen destination first to make sure it completely suits you. Locate other foreigners who live in the area and talk to them. Above all, make an educated decision about your future.

EARN $70,000 TAX FREE

This is not a gimmick. You can earn $70,000 without paying Uncle Sam the usual federal tax amounts. In order to do this, you need to either live and work in a foreign country for one year or spend 330 days of any 360-day period abroad. This does not include travel days.

In addition to the tax break, you might also qualify for a housing allowance, which may increase your total non-taxable income to over $90,000 in U.S. money. By putting the extra money you earn into savings, you can add that much more money to your retirement fund.

For more information on this income tax exclusion, get IRS publication #593: U.S. Citizens and Residents Abroad." Act fast, because this deal will probably not last forever.

As you can see, investing for the future doesn't have to be a painful decision. When you make a habit of it, saving money becomes a part of your life. What is much worse than going without a few extra luxuries when you are young, is to arrive at age 60 and discover you can't afford to live decently when you retire because you don't have any extra money on which to fall back.

IS YOUR PENSION PLAN IN TROUBLE?

One main reason people work so hard all their lives for the same company is to guarantee they have a pension when they retire. They may not like their job, but they'll have that wonderful stack of money available after age 65. After all, that was part of the deal. In exchange for 40 years of labor, the company promised to pay out a monthly check.

The problem is not all pension plans are in the condition necessary to pay all employees their pension benefits. The federal program which insures corporate pension plans is in deep trouble because of underfinancing.

Known as the Pension Benefit Guaranty Corporation (PBGC), this government sponsored insurance program protects the pensions of about 40 million American workers whose corporate pension plans are cancelled.

Termination of corporate pension plans occurs when the company has serious financial difficulty or declares bankruptcy.

The PBGC is radically underfinanced. This government corporation gets its money mainly from premiums collected from companies which sponsor an insured pension plan. Despite its assurances that everything is okay, the PBGC has an estimated $3 billion deficit. In 15 to 20 years, when the baby boom generation retires, that deficit could grow to $30 billion.

The PBGC's troubles are a result of the failure of some large companies to put away enough money to pay all the future pensions they promised their workers. Several small companies are also guilty of this oversight, which means PBGC has to pick up even more of the slack left by underfunded pensions.

Here are some other facts which you should know about pensions:

• Not all employer-sponsored pensions are in trouble.
What makes this such a serious problem is that most of the underfunding is done by a few large companies. The number of companies in trouble make up about one percent of PBGC's total clientele. However, the troubled companies make up about 75 percent of the total guaranteed benefits.

Most of these companies are in the auto, steel, and airline industries. In fact, Chrysler and General Motors are responsible for 53 percent of all underfunded guaranteed benefits.

• Not all company sponsored pension plans are underfunded.
The "defined-benefit" pension plan is the one underfinanced by corporations. These traditional pensions are supposed to make a monthly payment to you after you retire. Usually the amount you get depends on your salary and the number of years you worked at a company.

The other plans sponsored by companies—the 401(k) savings plans, the profit-sharing plans, and the money purchase plans—are not affected by underfunding. They are not protected by PBGC.

• Even if your company's pension plan is well-funded, your retirement income may not be in great shape.
More and more often, companies are giving up the idea of a traditional pension plan in favor of providing their workers with an insurance company annuity. An annuity is a monthly sum of money paid to you by an insurance company after you retire.

Insurance company annuities can be a good thing—as long as the sponsoring insurance company is in sound financial shape. If your sponsoring insurance company goes bankrupt, your next recourse is to go to your state guaranty association or fund. You usually end up with two alternatives—either you risk waiting several months or years to collect the full amount, or you collect now and take $.50 on the dollar.

• You can find out the financial condition of your company's pension plan.

Pay a visit to your pension plan's administrator and ask for a copy of your plan's annual report (Form 5500). Look for any mention of "unfunded-benefit liability." If you find it listed in the report along with a dollar figure, your pension plan is not fully financed by the company.

Also check the report for the plan's "funding ratio." If the percentage listed is less than 100 percent, your plan is underfinanced. The smaller the percentage, the greater the underfinancing.

• What you can do to make up the difference.
One of your options is simply to move on to another company where the pension plan is better financed. If this isn't possible, start using other ways to save for your retirement.

Contribute the maximum amount allowed to you employer-sponsored 401 (k) savings plan. Normally, your employer matches your contributions so you can end up with double what you put in. And you receive tax breaks along with compounding interest.

THE 401(k) PLAN
Like any other investment, the 401(k) plan takes some care and research before you invest in it. Even after investing in your employer's 401(k) plan, you need to stay on top of it to make sure the money is working to your best advantage. Here are some tips to make the most of 401(k) investments:

• Review a summary of the plan before signing up.
According to the law, the plan's sponsor is required to give you an easy-to-read description of the plan before you sign up. This summary includes information on whether your company will match your contributions, what percentage of your salary can go into your 401(k), what choices you have for investments, and how often your money can be redirected into other investments.

By knowing what is in the plan before you start, it will be easier for you to decide what other investments you might need outside your 401(k) plan to complete your retirement fund.

• Research you company's investment choices.
If your company has a good, small 401(k) plan, you should have at least four choices of investments to choose from—a money market fund, a fixed-income fund, a stock fund, and a balanced fund of stocks and bonds. Larger, more mature plans should offer at least eight to 10 choices to employees.

By researching the different opportunities, you are in a better position to realize when a plan is not in your best interests. If any of your plan's investments seem odd, ask your company's benefits person to request more information from the group who manages the plan.

Remember: selection of a 401(k) investment must be based entirely on the best interests of the participating employees. Any investment should give you the power to easily liquidate it, or to figure out its market value.

• Inform your company about your concerns.
If you feel your plan has limited or inappropriate investment choices, call the person who handles the benefits at your company. If you receive no response, write a letter to that person voicing your concerns.

Sometimes, however, companies are not willing to receive suggestions about changes in their 401(k) investment plans. If this is the case at your company, you need to remember that no one forced you to invest in the 401(k). You might end up having to decide which is more important to you—getting better investment choices, or keeping your job.

If it boils down to that, consider the future as well as the present. Is it worth remaining at a job whose 401(k) threatens your retirement, or is it okay for you to take your money and invest it elsewhere?

• Don't invest all your money into your company's stock.
This is without a doubt putting all your eggs into one basket. With all your money in one place, you end up completely dependent on the future of your company. If your company goes bankrupt and shuts its doors, you've just lost your job and your retirement fund.

The tough decision to invest everything in company stock comes about usually when a plan either gives you only the choice of investing in company stock or your employer agrees to match your contribution dollar for dollar if you invest in the company.

The way to avoid this sticky situation is to research where your company is going in the world of business. If you feel good about its future, it may very well be worth investing in company stock just to take advantage of your employer's matching amount.

However, move to a different investment as soon as you possibly can, usually after a certain amount of time has gone by. Before you sign anything, make sure you have the option of transferring the money tied up in company stock into some other investment.

• Before investing, compare the costs of your company's plan to other plans.
Sometimes plans end up costing a lot more over a long period of time than they are worth. Ask your plan's representative how much it costs annually to maintain your 401(k) plan, and who pays these administrative expenses.

Usually, annual expenses range from 0.3 to 0.7 percent of the total assets, with smaller plans costing even more. With the smaller plans, the employer often picks up the tab for these expenses. In the larger plans, the expenses are usually passed on to the employees. Once you find out what's what with your plan, you may decide that the annual expenses you pay to maintain your retirement fund are more than they are worth.

• Check the math at regular intervals.
It never hurts to double check any figures you receive on a 401(k) statement. You should receive a statement at least annually, but many company's send their employees statements quarterly or even monthly.

You need to check whether your contributions, your employer's contributions, and your investment earnings have all been properly credited to your account. Sometimes major mistakes can cost you thousands of dollars.

For example, one company had to pay some of its employees more than $100,000 to make up for money lost when the payroll department failed to follow employees' orders to invest in a stock which proceeded to m ke a lot of money. It's really worth the effort to keep track of your money.

• Your 401(k) does not have to go with you when you leave a job

By law, your 401(k) fu d can remain with your old company after you quit, as long as the balance is more than $3,500. Most employers do not inform their workers of this law possibly because they do not want to pay administrative costs to maintain retirement plans for former employees.

Maintaining a 401(k) at your old place of business may allow you to use any loan provisions, if the plan allows former employees to borrow money from the retirement plan.

Another option open to you is to rollover your money into your new employer's 401(k) plan, once you are eligible for the plan. If you feel uncomfortable with leaving the money at your former company, but have a wait of a year or more before you are eligible for the new plan, you can put your money into an IRA rollover account. This type of IRA is not subject to taxes or the usual IRA contribution limitations.

It isn't wise any longer to expect your employer or federal government to give you all the money you need to live comfortably upon retirement. The more you take charge of your own retirement plan, the better off you will be in the future when you really need the money.

CONCLUSION

By the time you get to this page, you are probably saying something like: "You know, you folks are absolutely correct! THIS IS THE MOST VALUABLE BOOK EVER WRITTEN!"

That's because somewhere within these pages you found something to make you richer, more healthy, happier, more fulfilled. Somewhere inthese pages, you found the key to an adventure you never thought possible in your "ordinary" lifestyle.

By this time, we hope the pages of this book are all dog-eared and tattered, filled with underlined paragraphs or highlighted with bright-colored ink. That's the way to gain the fullest advantage of the information which has been presented here.

You see, without you, this book is not complete. In fact, without you, this manuscript could never live up to its name, The Most Valuable Book Ever Written. Why? Because ideas and information in and of themselves are just that -- ideas and information lying dormant, trapped within a prison of ordinary ink and paper.

You are the one who has to TRANSFORM ideas and information into ACTION. The best financial plan in the world will not imrpove your bottom line until you actually take that plan and make is a reality in your daily life! A weight loss plan will not shed the pounds from your body until you actually practice that plan in your real life.

Get the picture? We, the authors of this book, see ourselves in partnership with you. We've labored for months putting this book together so that you can have all the tools you need to make real, positive changes in your life. We provide the answers; it's up to you pick up those answers and run with them.

Like a prospector exploring the depths and streams of a mineral rich mountainside for gold, you can plunge into this book again and again, mining for valuable bits of information which you can bring out into reality to enrich your life with.

We hope you will delve back into this book many times, each time finding something new and wonderful. Happy prospecting!

FREE REPORTS

Banks are the ideal place for all of your financial activities, right? Wrong!

Property insurance

You are probably paying twice as much for the property insurance on your house if your mortgage insurance is handled by your bank or mortgage company.

Call your bank or mortgage company and ask to see your policy, your premium statement, and the coverage on your property. Then shop around. You'll probably be pleasantly surprised to find the same coverage for about 1/2 what you are now paying.

Mutual funds

The quality of funds and investment advise is questionable at banks. Some bank-brokerages have inexperienced investment advisers - many confine their recommendations to just a few funds or push their own in-house mutuals.

Although it may be convenient to do your investing at your bank, it may cost you. Remember, these are the people who brought you 3% CDs!

How to deduct losses on your boat

You can deduct losses on your boat if your set it up as a sideline business.

Sideline business are a favorite target of the IRS, so you will have to be very careful and very professional in establishing your business.
SuggestionsBanks are the ideal place for all of your financial

activities, right? Wrong!

Property insurance

You are probably paying twice as much for the property insurance on your house if your mortgage insurance is handled by your bank or mortgage company.

Call your bank or mortgage company and ask to see your policy, your premium statement, and the coverage on your property. Then shop around. You'll probably be pleasantly surprised to find the same coverage for about 1/2 what you are now paying.

Mutual funds

The quality of funds and investment advise is questionable at banks. Some bank-brokerages have inexperienced investment advisers - many confine their recommendations to just a few funds or push their own in-house mutuals.

Although it may be convenient to do your investing at your bank, it may cost you. Remember, these are the people who brought you 3% CDs!

How to deduct losses on your boat

You can deduct losses on your boat if your set it up as a sideline business.

Sideline business are a favorite target of the IRS, so you will have to be very careful and very professional in establishing your business.
SuggestionsBanks are the ideal place for all of your financial activities, right? Wrong!

Property insurance

You are probably paying twice as much for the property insurance on your house if your mortgage insurance is handled by your bank or mortgage company.

Call your bank or mortgage company and ask to see your policy, your premium statement, and the coverage on your property. Then shop around. You'll probably be pleasantly surprised to find the same coverage for about 1/2 what you are now paying.

Mutual funds

The quality of funds and investment advise is questionable at banks. Some bank-brokerages have inexperienced investment advisers - many confine their recommendations to just a few funds or push their own in-house mutuals.

Although it may be convenient to do your investing at your bank, it may cost you. Remember, these are the people who brought you 3% CDs!

How to deduct losses on your boat

You can deduct losses on your boat if your set it up as a sideline business.

Sideline business are a favorite target of the IRS, so you will have to be very careful and very professional in establishing your business.
Suggestions

FREE REPORTS

BANKS

Banks are the ideal place for all of your financial activities, right? Wrong!

Property insurance

You are probably paying twice as much for the property insurance on your house if your mortgage insurance is handled by your bank or mortgage company.

Call your bank or mortgage company and ask to see your policy, your premium statement, and the coverage on your property. Then shop around. You'll probably be pleasantly surprised to find the same coverage for about 1/2 of what you are now paying.

Mutual funds

The quality of funds and investment advise is questionable at banks. Some bank-brokerages have inexperienced investment advisers - many confine their recommendations to just a few funds or push their own in-house mutuals.

Although it may be convenient to do your investing at your bank, it may cost you. Remember, these are the people who brought you 3% CDs!

How to deduct losses on your boat

You can deduct losses on your boat if you set it up as a sideline business.

Sideline business are a favorite target of the IRS, so you will have to be very careful and very professional in establishing your business.

Suggestions

Research the business and work up realistic financial projections and keep records before entering your business.

Review your projections annually and keep records of the review.

Conduct your business in a professional manner. Hire a chartering agency, hold promotions, show your expected revenues to at least equal expenses - that you're genuinely attempting to make a profit.

If you can prove that this is a genuine business and not an attempt to deduct hobby or recreational activities, you can legally deduct the losses on your boat.

CHILDREN'S TAX-FREE EARNINGS

Children can only earn $3,700 a year tax-free, right? Wrong!
If your children are working in your business, you can place the maximum contribution for each in the 401K plan. The maximum contribution is almost $9,000 per employee based on the employee's gross income earned.

HIGH CHOLESTEROL

High cholesterol can sneak up on you. You can feel just fine and still have high cholesterol which puts you at risk for heart disease.

So how do you know if you have a cholesterol problem. Your lifestyle can give you a clue.

Checking your cholesterol life-style

(1)   Do you eat a lot of prepared, convenience, or fast food?
(2)   Do you eat butter, whole milk, and cheese?
(3)   Do you eat a lot of steaks, chops, ribs, and rib roasts?
(4)   Do you eat a lot of fried foods?
(5)   Do you eat a lot of gravies and sauces?
(6)   Are you a few pounds overweight?
(7)   Do you find you don't make time to exercise?

The more "yes" answers you have, the greater your risk of having high cholesterol - and the more important it is for you to have your cholesterol level checked. Also, the greater the benefits to you if you follow a cholesterol reducing program.

Why do we have cholesterol anyway?

It's most important job is to help carry fat through your bloodstream. This works pretty good most of the time, but when you eat too much fat, too much cholesterol may accumulate. Then serious problems like heart attacks can occur.

Where does cholesterol come from?

Your liver makes most of your cholesterol to help carry fat to other parts of your body for energy (or to store on your hips or belly or other undesirable storage spots). But some of your cholesterol comes from eating high cholesterol foods.

Three types of cholesterol

Three? Yes, three. But it isn't all bad news! The three kinds are: very low-density lipoprotein (VLDL), low-density lipoprotein (LDL), and high density lipoprotein (HDL).

VLDL carries fat from the liver to other parts of your body. After it unloads the fat, it becomes LDL.

LDL is called "bad" cholesterol because pieces of it can become stuck to blood vessel walls.

HDL is called "good" cholesterol because it finds the stuck LDL and brings it back to the liver.

What happens when you eat too much fat?

Your liver makes extra VLDLs to carry it. More LDL pieces get stuck. If there aren't enough HDLs to rescue them all blood vessels may become blocked.

How does quitting smoking help?

Smoking lowers your HDL (your good cholesterol) and increases your risks of heart attack, stroke, and cancer. If you quit smoking, your level of good cholesterol will be higher.

How does exercise help?

A regular aerobic exercise program helps to raise your HDL (your good cholesterol) and also helps you loose weight. Aerobic exercise includes things like walking, swimming, and jogging. You should exercise at least four times a week for a half hour each time.

What does weight have to do with it?

If you weigh too much, your body will store more fat and cholesterol causing your blood cholesterol level to rise.

Fat has 9 calories per gram, protein has 4 calories per gram, and starches have 4 calories per gram. Because fat has the most calories per gram, the quickest way to loose weight is to reduce the amount of fats you eat.

The most effective way to reduce your cholesterol level

Changing your diet is probably the most effective way to reduce your cholesterol level.

Less fat

The most helpful change is to the lower the amount of fat you eat. Your goal is to limit fats to one-third of your total caloric intake. You will want to avoid both the obvious fats, such as fatty meats and whole milk, and the hidden fats in processed foods.

Read labels to choose low fat foods. Labels list ingredients by weight. A product is likely to be high in fat if fats and/or oils are listed near the top of the ingredient list or if several fat ingredients are listed. Another test for processed foods is in calories. Take the number of grams of fat times 9 (each gram of fat has 9 calories). If the answer is equal to more than 1/3 of the total calories in the product, it is higher in fat than your total diet should be.

More fiber

Eat more fiber. Soluble fiber (found in oats, beans, and fruit) lowers your cholesterol level by keeping the cholesterol you eat from being absorbed by your body.

Less cholesterol

Limit high cholesterol foods in your diet - eat less eggs and meat.

More starches

Starches such as grains, beans, and root vegetables aren't fattening and can reduce your cholesterol level.

Caffeine and alcohol

Both caffeine and alcohol can raise your cholesterol level by raising the fat levels in your blood. Your limit should be two cups of coffee and two alcoholic beverages per day.

Three kinds of fat

Yes, three. Nothing is easy in this life! The three types are monounsaturated, polyunsaturated, and saturated. Use less saturated fat and use monounsaturated and polyunsaturated instead.

Monounsaturated fat is olive oil and canola oil. These fats lower LDL (bad cholesterol) without lowering HDL (good cholesterol). This is why some doctors recommend increasing your intake of monounsaturated fats.

Polyunsaturated fat is safflower, sunflower, or corn oil. It may lower both good and bad cholesterol so your intake of these fats should be carefully monitored, but it is preferable to saturated fat.

Saturated fat should be avoided. This is the category of butter, lard, and meat. It also includes coconut oil, palm oil, and "partially hydrogenated" oil. Many processed foods contain these oils. Too much saturated fat can raise you cholesterol level.

CREATIVITY WITHOUT DRUGS

Creativity of any kind begins with ideas - new, novel, innovative ideas. The great work of art, the wonderful solution to a problem, the terrific book, the dandy invention are all merely applications of ideas. All creativity begins with creative thinking. It's as simple as that.

Creative thinking

Right. But how do you achieve creative thinking? How do you come up with these innovative ideas?

Creative thinking may mean simply the realization that there's no particular virtue in doing things the way they've always been done. — Rudolf Flesch

Okay, that's easy enough. You accept the fact that the conventional way may not be the only way - or even the best way. But at that point, you're only half-way there. You still need to come up with an unconventional way - a new and different way. How do you do it?

You don't need drugs

You don't need drugs to think creatively. You just need to change the way you think. The process of creative thinking can be learned. But if you're going to change the way you think, learn a new way to think, you need to know how thinking is done.

An invisible activity

Since thinking is an invisible activity, you can't see it. Well, yes, you can see people wrinkle their foreheads or scratch their heads. But that's not really thinking, just indications that thinking is going on. On the other hand, wrinkled foreheads and itchy scalp could just mean an impending migraine or a case of dandruff. And the thinking you do yourself is probably so automatic that you really aren't aware of how you do it.

Results of thinking

Okay, but you can see great works of art, dandy inventions, fantastic books, beautiful architecture, and complicated computer equipment. These things, though, are results of thinking. You can see the results but not the process itself.

The invisible process

To learn to be a creative thinker, you must become aware of the process, of what you do when you think.

The first step to awareness is to recognize that you use two types of thinking. Edward de Bono, an expert on thinking, labels them vertical and lateral thinking.

Stepping logically down the path

Vertical thinking is "conventional" thinking - the kind we are most familiar with because we use it most. This is the logical step-by-step approach that chooses the most logical path to the solution of a problem. And vertical thinking makes judgements of right or wrong at each step of that path.

As you can see, vertical thinking takes only logical paths. It shuts off pathways or ideas right at the entrance gate if they don't seem logical. And at any step along the way, it makes logical judgements that slam a gates, shutting off further exploration in other directions.

Now logic is wonderful, but sometimes what works may be contrary to what seems obvious or logical.

Skipping illogically down the path

Lateral thinking, on the other hand, suspends judgement, and approaches ideas with humor, insight, and creativity. It goes skipping down unlikely paths, exploring and speculating. It's unafraid to experiment with the unusual and bizarre. It looks at alternatives. It explores paths that may seem silly.

Lateral thinking takes you off the beaten path and may lead you to an insight, a new and innovative concept, or a restructuring of the problem itself. It closes no gates. As you can see, lateral thinking opens the way to exploring innovative and unusual ideas - creativity.

Throwing logic to the winds

Hold it! I'm not advocating throwing logic to the winds — just suspending it sometimes.

You need both kinds of thinking. Lateral thinking will help you generate new ideas; vertical thinking will help you develop those new ideas into workable concepts.

Be a screwball!

There is a correlation between the creative and "the screwball." So we must suffer the screwball gladly.— Kingman Brewster

Loosen up! Be a screwball. Get silly. Get crazy. Try to go beyond the obvious. That's where creative ideas come from.

Suspend your judgement of new methods and approaches. Let your imagination run rampant. Explore the possibilities of ideas that may seem silly or downright stupid. Even if some ideas seem foolish, follow them through in your mind.

The thoroughly logical mind

If you have a thoroughly logical mind, it will take some time and practice to pursue screwball ideas. But you can train yourself to think creatively - and you don't need drugs. Loosen up! Your thought processes are invisible - no one will know the illogical (embarrassing?) paths they follow.

Save on credit card interest

Credit cards are billed out on a cycle - the cycle depends upon the card you use.

Make a quick call and find out what your billing cycle is and pay your card BEFORE the interest is computed. Just one quick call and you save big bucks!

DIABETES

To understand what goes wrong when you have diabetes, you need to know how your body worked before the condition developed.

Before diabetes

Your body changed food into sugar and sent it into the blood. Insulin carried the sugar out of the blood and into the cells. The cells burned the sugar to make energy.

The insulin also left a little sugar behind in the blood - a back-up supply. This "blood sugar" level can be measured with a blood test. Before diabetes your insulin kept your blood sugar in the safe range.

With diabetes

Your insulin doesn't work right and too much sugar stays in your blood. This is "high blood sugar". With diabetes, your blood sugar will always want to go too high because your insulin isn't doing its job right.

Type I diabetes

Your body has stopped making insulin. Your body still changes food into sugar and sends it into the blood. But your body isn't making insulin anymore, so there is no insulin to carry the sugar to the cells. Your cells are starving for sugar to burn. They can't make energy. Since the sugar isn't being carried out of your blood to the cells, your blood sugar goes too high.

Type II diabetes

Your body is making insulin but it isn't working right - it's "tired". Your body still changes food into sugar and sends it into the blood. But your tired insulin isn't working fast enough. Your cells are not getting some sugar but not enough.

Since the sugar isn't being carried out of your blood fast enough, your blood sugar goes too high.

Symptoms

High blood sugar can make you tired, thirsty, and hungry all of the time. Other symptoms can include blurred vision, numbness in feet, hands, and legs, slow-healing wounds, clogged blood vessels and heart problems, kidney problems, and (in Type II) weight gain.

Treatment

Although there is still no cure for diabetes, you can learn to live with it and keep it under control. Your goal, of course is to keep your blood sugar level within the safe range.

Controlling Type I

Controlling Type I diabetes requires a food plan and an exercise plan. Since your body is no longer producing insulin, it also requires insulin.

Controlling Type II

Controlling Type II diabetes also requires a food and exercise plan. In addition, weight and maintenance are important. Since you do have insulin, even though it isn't working properly, you may not need insulin. You may be able to keep it under control naturally.

What makes blood sugar go up

Food: When your body changes food into sugar, your blood sugar goes up. Some foods, like sweets, change very fast. Your tired insulin has trouble when your blood sugar rises too fast. It may not be able to get the sugar out your blood and into your cells fast enough to avoid problems.

It's better if your blood sugar goes up slowly so your tired insulin has time to do the job. Foods like bread, vegetables, and fruit change to sugar more slowly.

Stress: Stress includes things like fear, lack of sleep, worry, anger, rapid weight loss, and growth spurts. You need extra energy to handle stress. Your body reacts by making extra sugar. Your tired insulin may not be able to work fast enough to get this sugar out of your blood and into your cells to keep your blood sugar within the safe range.

Illness: Sickness is also stress on your body. It makes your blood sugar go up like other stress.

What makes blood sugar go down

Exercise: When you exercise, your cells burn more sugar and your blood sugar goes down. Exercise also helps your insulin work better.

Diabetes pills: Diabetes pills are not insulin, but they perk up your tired insulin - help it to work better.

Insulin: Injecting insulin is like calling in temporary reinforcement troops. This insulin will work alongside your insulin to get the job done. These troops are just temporary, though. After a few hours, they get tired and leave.

Low blood sugar

Low blood sugar can also be a problem when you have diabetes. Blood sugar levels can drop very fast and sometimes without warning if:
    (1) You don't eat enough or skip a meal.
    (2) You take too much insulin or too large a dose of
         diabetes pills.
    (3) You exercised a lot and forgot to eat a snack.

The signs of low blood sugar

Low blood sugar may make you feel nervous, shaky, confused, dizzy, irritable or angry, dizzy, sweaty, or hungry. Treat it quickly or you may pass out. It can get worse very fast.

What to do for low blood sugar
    (1) Eat or drink something sugary - fast.
    (2) Wait five minutes.
    (3) Check your blood sugar.
    (4) If it's still low, eat a snack - a carbohydrate
         with a protein.

(5) Rest until you feel better,
(6) After 30 minutes, check your blood sugar again.

"The Boy Scout motto"

Diabetics, like Boy Scouts, should always be prepared. Always carry something sugary with you and keep a snack pack in your car.

How can you control your blood sugar level

Food: You need carbohydrates and proteins each time you eat. Vegetables, fruit, and grains are good sources of carbohydrates. Lean meats and low-fat dairy products are protein sources. Beans and dairy products are great because they provide both carbohydrates and protein.

Avoid sweet, sugary things and fats. Avoid or limit alcohol.

Exercise: Combined with a sensible diet, regular aerobic exercise can be the key to controlling diabetes. Take 45. All you need is 45 minutes of walking each day. That's it - just 45 minutes of walking briskly while swinging your arms - and it's natural and cost free. A very easy walking program often can actually control Type II diabetes without medication or insulin injections.
How does walking perform this miracle? First, it burns some of the sugar. Second, it "wakes up" your tired insulin.

In addition, it helps you to lower and maintain your weight, lower your cholesterol, and reduce stress - all of which are important in the control of diabetes.

Scheduling your walking is very important. The benefits of walking last for about 24 hours, so you must walk every day and at about the same time each day.

Sensible precautions

When you have diabetes, you must be very careful with your feet since your inhibited circulation makes them susceptible to infections. So before you begin your walking program, get proper, comfortable footwear. Carry or wear diabetes identification - a card, necklace, or bracelet. Carry a snack pack including extra fluids, hard candies, and crackers and cheese. If you have Typel diabetes, carry a Glucagon Kit.

When not to exercise

As important as walking is, there are times you shouldn't do it. When: you don't feel well, you have pain, your blood sugar is above 240, your blood sugar is below 60, you have keytones in your urine, your insulin is peaking and you haven't yet eaten, it's too hot or too humid, or your doctor says no.

Chromium picolinate

Chromium is an essential element of nutrition. It facilitates the action of insulin, glucose, protein, and fat. Two hundred micrograms of chromium per day has been shown to lower glucose levels by 18% and glycosylated hemoglobin by 10%.

Vitamin E and diabetes complications.
Complications of diabetes in the heart, eyes, kidneys, nervous system, and feet are linked to cholesterol blockages in the blood vessels. Recent studies indicate that vitamin E may help in preventing these complications by intercepting cholesterol and unstable oxygen molecules that damage artery walls.

Supplements of vitamin A, B6, C, and niacin are also recommended.

Preventing Infections and Diseases

The Hospital Infection

When you are hospitalized, you don't have to worry about being exposed to infections and diseases, right? Wrong. Although hospitals don't want you to know about it, many patients get staph infection while in the hospital - an extremely serious and contagious infection that's difficult to treat.

How do you get it?

Because staph infection is very contagious, it's easily spread from patient to patient by personnel who neglect to wash their hands when entering and leaving a room.

Reduce your risk of contracting staph infection by insisting that all the caretakers who enter your room wash their hands before administering to your needs.

How often are you ill?

In the United States, the average person has two or more short and severe illnesses each year. These infectious diseases are caused by many kinds of germs including bacteria, viruses, and protozoa.

Protect your home from disease

Many diseases and infections, even serious ones, can be prevented by simple health practices within the home. Preventative measures include proper nutrition, rest, and cleanliness.

Proper nutrition and rest

Get proper nutrition and rest. Both are important to good health. Some diseases like scurvy and rickets are the direct result of nutritional deficiency. In addition, lack of nutrition and rest can cause disease indirectly by lowering the body's resistance to germs and bacteria that normally do no harm.

Your body requires some 40 nutrients to maintain health. That's a lot to keep track of. But you don't have to keep a chart of each. Just eating a variety of foods from the four basic food groups should provide you with the nutrients you need.

The groups are:

(1) Fruits and vegetables
(2) Grain products
(3) Dairy products
(4) Legumes, nuts, seeds, meat, poultry, fish, eggs

Cleanliness can protect you from disease and infection. In addition to nutrition and rest, cleanliness is extremely important in avoiding and preventing the spread of disease. Disinfecting is particularly important if a member of your household is ill.

Disinfecting the sick room

Preparations of carbolic acid, or phenol, can be used to sterilize contaminated clothing, utensels, bathroom, etc. To prepare a disinfecting solution of carbolic acid, use one part carbolic acid to 20 parts water.

Is your kitchen the source of disease?

In the modern busy household, dishes often are not washed after every meal. Bacteria multiplies rapidly on dirty dishes and can create health problems.

A common household item that can be used for disinfecting dishes is a chlorine bleach - regular household bleach! Just add a few cents worth of bleach along with your detergent to your dish water to disinfect dishes and utensils.

Also use this solution for cleaning counters and cutting boards after handling raw meat and poultry to prevent trichinosis and salmonella contamination. An empty squeeze-type dish detergent bottle makes a handy dispenser. Just squeeze in a bit of bleach when you do your dishes. Disinfectants are powerful chemicals. Keep them out of reach of children.

Fight back and win

When you have a problem with real estate, insurance, doctors, and lawyers, often a simple phone call will get you satisfaction. For problems with real estate, call your State Association of Realtors. For insurance problems, call your State Insurance Department.

For a problem with doctors, call your state office of the American Medical Association. If your problem is with lawyers, call your State Bar Association or your state Attorney General.

Over Fifty Hobby and Craft Items You can Get FREE!

Free Stuff

You can get an amazing number of free things just for asking - if you know who to write to. Below are the addresses for over fifty items you can get absolutely free. All you have to do is write and ask for them!

Keep in mind: Postal regulations require that you put your return address on the envelope. It may take up to eight weeks before you get the item. The companies reserve the right to change or withdraw the offer. Use postcards whenever possible. State what item it is that you're requesting.

Sample request:
Please send me your free booklet entitled "Invite Wildlife To Your Backyard." Thank you.

Invite Wildlife to Your Backyard
National Wildlife Federation
1412 16 St NW
Washington, CD 20030

Invite Birds to Your Home
USDA
Box 2890 Washington, DC 20012

Phun Phelt
Eastman Kodak
343 State Street
Rochester, NY 14650

Pellon Co.
Dept FT
119 W 40th St
NY, NY 10018

How You Can Make Paper
American Paper Inst.
260 Madison Ave.
Hartford, CT 06156

Lilles, Lillies, and More Lillies
Rex Bulb Farms
Po Box 774
Port Tonsend, WA 98368

Planting Guide
Miller Nurseries
Dpt. 705
West Lake RD
Canandalgua, NY 14424

Crafts and More Crafts
Consumer Services, Johnson
Wax
1525 Howe St
Racine, WI 53403

Sewing Guide - Thread
Sewing Guide - Stitches
Sewing Guide - Seams
Sewing Guide - Hems
All From:
Belfding - Lilly Co.
Consumer Information
PO Box 88
Shelby, NC. 28151

Speedball Pen Lettering
Charts
Hunt Mfg.
Speedball Rd
Statesville, NC 28677

Free Golf Pamphlets
Golf Digest
297 Westport Ave
Norwalk, CT 06856

Family Crafts Boutique
(include stamped self-
addressed envelope)
Borden Consumer Products

Information Center
PO Box 157
Hilliard, OH 43026

Introducing Your Children to
Wildlife
Defenders of Wildlife
PO Box 3800
Washington, DC 20007

Archery Made Easy
Ben Pearson, Inc
Pine Bluff, AR 71601

Introduction to Scale Model
Railroading
Kalmbach Publishing Co.
2027 Crossroads Circle
Waotesha, WI 53186

How to Make Play Clay
Play Clay
Arm and Hommer
PO Box 369
Piscataway, NJ 08854

Basic Canoeing
Grumman Boats
Marathon, NY 13803

Chinese Calligraphy
Chinese Info Service
159 Lexington Ave
New York, NY 10016

Fishing Tips
Cisco Kid Tackle
2630 NW First Ave
Boca Raton, FL 33432

How to Cure Golf's Six Most
Common Faults

Golf Digest
PO Box 5350
Norwalk, CT 06856

How to Panel a Room
Masonite Corp
PO Box 311
Towanda, PA 18848

Mix'n Make - Glue Dough
Mix'n Make - Glue Paint
Consumer Products Division,
Borden Chemical
180 E Broad St
Columbus, OH 43215

Recipe Cards
Argo & Kingsford's Recipe
Cards
PO Box 307VP
Coventry, CT 06238

Perdue Cookbook
PO Box 1537
Salisbury, MD 21802

How to Improve Your TV &
FM Reception
Channel Master
Division of Avnet, Inc.
Ellenville, NY 12428

Training Riding Horses,
American Quarter Horse
Assn.
PO Box 200
Amarillo, TX 79105

Don't Make Waves (boating)
State Farm Public Relations
1 State Farm Plaza Dept R
Bloomington, IL 61701

How to Play Chess
Dover Publications
31 E 2nd St
Mineola, NY 11501

Year-Round Gardening With a
Greenhouse #538K (Put
FREE on Outside of
Envelope)
Consumer Information
Pueblo, CO 81009

Birdwatching
Wildlife Federation
1412 16th St NW
Washington, DC 20036

Postage Stamp Booklets
US Postal Servvice
Consumer Affairs Dept.
Washington, DC 20260

What Do You Know About the
Big Dipper?
How to Start a Nature Club
Both from:
National Wildlife Federation
1412 16th St NW
Washington, DC 20036

Throw a Hawaiian Luau
Del Monte Luau Booklet Offer
PO Box 9009
Clinton, IA 52732

A Tale of Two Bike Riders
Employers Insurance of
Wausau
PO Box 150
Wausau, WI 54401

Unusual Thimble Catalog
The Collector's Choice
1313 S Killian Dr.
Lake Park, FL 60196

Official Rules for Horseshoe
Pitching
National Assoc. of Horseshoe
Pitchers
Horeseshoe Pitchers Digest
13074 Solfisburg Ave
Aurora, IL 60505

Window Idea Booklet
Pella Windows Co.
100 Main St
Pella, IA 50219

Emergency Telephone
Number Card
Travelers Insurance
Women's Info Bureau
One Tower Square
Hartford, CT 06115

Paneling Ideas
Eastern Hardboard
PO Box 311
Towanda, PA 18848

The Anderson Home
Remodeling Series
Anderson Co.
Bayport, MN 55003

How to Roller Skate
4400-58 West Lake St
Garfield Park St N
Chicago, IL 60624

How To Grow An Organic
Garden in a Nutshell

Organic Gardening & Farming
33 E Minor St
Emmaus, PA 18049

Should We Hunt?
National Wildlife
1412 16th St NW
Washington, DC 20036

Build a Greenhouse Catalog
Peter Reimuller
PO Box 2666 Dept 7-A
Santa Cruz, CA 95063

Printing Methods # AT-13
Eastman Kodak Co.
343 State St
Rochester, NY 14650

Point Count Bidding (include
stamped self-addressed
envelope)
U.S. Postal Service
Director of Advertising
475 L'Enfant Plaza, West
Washington, DC 20260

Free C-B Dictionary
American Trucking Assn
Education Section
430 1st St SE
Washington, DC 20003

Have a Hobby Booklets
(include stamped self-
addressed envelope)
Hobby Industry Assn
319 East 54th St
Elmwood Park, NJ 07407

Learn How to Wallpaper
(include stamped self-

addressed envelope)
Red Devil Tools
PO Box "W"
Union, NJ 07083

How to Play Better Doubles
(include stamped self-
addressed envelope)
Tennis Magazine
297 Westport Ave
Norwalk, CT 06856

Bicycle Safety Posters
U.S. Consumer Product
Safety Commission
Washington, DC 20207

Christmas Carols (with words
and music)
John Hancock Mutual Life
Insurance
PO Box 111
Boston, MA 02117

Elderhostel Catalog (for senior
citizen travelers)
Elderhostel
100 Boylston St
Boston, MA 02116

100 Free Foreign Stamps
Littleton Stamp Co
Dept G
Littleton, NH 03561

Free Plastic 6-inch Ruler
(include stamped self-
addressed envelope)
ILGWU
Union Labe Dept
275 Seventh Ave, 5th Floor
New York, NY 10001

Doll Talk (mini magazine)
Kimport Dolls
PO Box 495
Independence, MO 64051-
0495

UNCLE SAM'S BARGAINS

Did you ever wish for a rich and generous uncle? Well, you have one - old Uncle Sam.

GOVERNMENT AUCTIONS

Uncle Sam offers millions of dollars worth of property and goods at unbelievably low prices throughout the year - every year. You can buy everything from furniture to automobiles dirt cheap. The government spends very little money on advertising these bargains, so few people know of them. How can you get your share of the bargains?

Contact the offices below for up-to-date information:

Sales of surplus Federal property are held at government buildings throughout the country. Available merchandise at these sales include: automobiles, furniture, office equipment, kitchen equipment, and other valuable items.

    Contact:
    General Services Administration
    Surplus Sales Branch
    7th and D Streets SW
    Washington, DC 20407

    General Services Administration
    Surplus Sales Branch
    75 Spring Street
    Atlanta, Ga 30303

    General Services Administration
    Surplus Sales Branch
    525 market Street
    San Francisco, CA 94105

IRS

Who wouldn't like to get back a little something from this office? Well, here's your chance. The IRS holds regular auctions to liquidate items - real estate, cars, furniture, boats, and more -

seized from businesses and individuals who failed to pay their taxes.

Contact: your local Internal Revenue Service, Collection Division Office. Ask them to put you on their auction mailing list.

SMALL BUSINESS ADMINISTRATION (SBA)

When the Small Business Administration forecloses on business loans, they end up with entire businesses. You could end up owning a small business! Or you may want to bid on business supplies, goods, machinery, and other items.

Look in larger newspapers in the Classified Section under Bids and Proposals, or Contact: the Liquidation Officer at your local SBA office or U.S. Small Business Administration, General Agency Information, 1441 L Street NW, Washington, DC 20416.

U.S. CUSTOMS SERVICE

A wide variety of consumer goods are seized every year. About once a year they are auctioned through local or regional customs offices.

Contact: your local Customs Office or U.S. Customs Service, P.O. Box 7118, Washington, DC 20044.

POSTAL SERVICE

The Postal Service auctions unclaimed merchandise and surplus office equipment. The merchandise includes a lot of books and a large variety of other interesting items.

Contact: your local Post Office and ask for the closest Dead Parcel Office or the U.S. Postal Service, 475 L'Enfant Plaza, West Building, Washington, DC 20260 202-523-2253

INTERESTED IN HOMES OR LAND?

Perhaps you are more interested in homes or land than in goods. Well, Uncle Sam has those at bargain prices, too. For information on the following, call the phone number listed or Contact: Urban

Homesteading Division, Office of Urban Rehabilitation and Community Reinvestment, Community Planning and Development, Department of Housing and Urban Development, 451 7th St. SW, Rm 7168, Washington, DC 20410

Lottery

The Urban Homesteading Program makes government defaulted properties available for $1.00 through a lottery. You must bring the property up to minimum health and safety standards within 36 months and live there for at least 5 years. Phone 202-755-5324

Homes at reasonable prices

The Department of Housing and Urban Development also offers homes acquired by HUD Properties Disposition Department through FHA and VA loan default. Phone: 202-755-5324

Homes for $1.00
The department of Housing and Urban Development turns some run-down homes over to local communities to sell to low-income families. Usually they can be purchased for $1.00. Find out if your community is participating in this program and if you qualify.
Phone: 202-755-8702 or 202-755-6880

IMPOTENCE

A failure to achieve or maintain an erection in at least 25 percent of attempts is called impotence. As you can see, an occasional inability to achieve or maintain an erection is not classified as impotency.

However, an understanding of the causes and remedies for impotency can be of help with the occasional problem, too.

Nearly every man

Whether they admit it to each other or not, nearly every man has had difficulty achieving or maintaining an erection at one time or another. So don't panic if an erection isn't happening every time you expect it to. Your masculinity is NOT threatened, even if you feel like it is.

Your reaction is important

The episode itself is not as important as how you react to it. If you worry about it and about future performance, you are almost certain to intensify the problem.

Some causes

An occasional episode of inability to gain an erection can stem from several different things - tiredness, too much to drink, stress, drugs.

Talk to your partner

It's important to talk with your partner about it. Remember this is her problem, too. A worried or embarrassed silence will certainly not help anything and may devastate your relationship.

Talk about the importance of your relationship. Explain that nearly every man has this problem occasionally. Reassure your partner. She may feel her femininity is threatened. If she is reassured, she can be a greater support to you.

Don't try to change how she feels. Trying to change how she feels will add to your frustration. Just try to understand how she feels.

Causes and remedies

Now, let's examine some of the causes impotency and some of the things you can do to enjoy longer and better sex.

Tired?

As we said before, tiredness can be a cause of problems. The remedy? Get some rest. Don't try to force your tired body to perform.

Alcohol Causes Problems

Even a couple of drinks can cause problems. Alcohol may increase your desire, but it's a depressant and decreases your performance. Continuous use of alcohol can cause liver damage. This, in turn, creates an excess of female hormones in your body. With an improper balance of hormones, you can expect to have erection problems.

Stress

Is stress the culprit? Walking every day can lessen stress. Walking brings about physiological changes in your body that help to relax you.

Drugs

Drugs - recreational, prescription, and over-the-counter drugs - can sometimes cause problems. Avoid cocaine, heroin, marijuana, and other recreational drugs. Blood pressure pills, tranquilizers, antidepressants, diuretics, heart medications, arthritis medications, antihistamines and many other prescription medications can cause impotence. Over-the-counter medical preparations that could be the cause are: antihistimines, diuretics, sedatives and others.

If you are taking any drugs regularly, check with your doctor or pharmacist. If they feel your medications could be causing the problem, they may be able to decrease your dosage or change you to a different drug. DO NOT ADJUST YOUR MEDICATION WITHOUT CONSULTING YOUR DOCTOR.

Anxiety

If you are afraid of failure, your body may react by producing excessive amounts of a hormone called norepinephrine causing an inability to achieve an erection.

A good way to relax is to make an agreement with your partner to engage in sex play without worrying about whether it will end in intercourse. Just plan for a session of sensual fun and games.

Time

As you get older, you may need a little more time. Relax. Give yourself plenty of time.

Refraction

Your refraction period - the time from ejaculation until you can again achieve an erection - also increases with age. An increased refraction time is not a sign of impotency.

Nicotine

Nicotine is a blood vessel constrictor. Since penile erection depends on blood flow, the use of nicotine could cause problems.

Pain

Your body reacts to pain by producing opiates. This can cause an inability to achieve an erection. All you can do is wait until you are feeling better.

Stimulants

Coffee and soda pop often contain a great deal of caffeine - a stimulant. Switch to the decaffeinated variety of your favorite beverage.

Depression

Depression can affect sexual performance. This is a touchy situation since most anti-depressants can decrease potency.
Bupropion hydrochloride, however, is an anti-depressant that increases sexual desire and functioning. If you are depressed or are now taking anti-depressants, ask your doctor about this drug.

What you eat

Whatever affects the blood flow in your arteries also affects the blood flow to your penis. Erections depend upon blood flow. So, watch what you eat. Go on a low-cholesterol, low-fat, cardiac diet. A program for reducing your risk of heart attack will also benefit your sex life.

Niacin

Niacin, an over-the-counter vitamin, helps to increase blood circulation and reduce cholesterol. A great aid to longer and better sex!

Exercise

Exercise is good for your circulation, reduces stress, and tones up your body. But don't exercise too much - if you get carried away with exercising your body will produce opiates like it does when you are in pain. This lessens your ability to achieve an erection.

External vacuum devise

This is a devise to help you achieve an erection. It does not require drugs or surgery. It is merely a small hand held pump with a cylinder. You slip the cylinder over your penis sealing it against your body. When you pump, a vacuum is created drawing blood into the penis, and an erection is formed. You slip a latex ring onto the base of your penis before removing the cylinder - the erection is maintained by the ring. It only takes a couple of minutes and you are ready for intercourse. The devise is available by prescription.

Injection

Injections of prostaglandin E1, papaverine, or phentolamine are effective for impotence and premature ejaculation. They stimulate the blood flow into your penis and produce an instant erection. Your erection can last from 10 minutes to two hours - it depends on the dosage - regardless of how many times you ejaculate.

Reverse roles

Premature ejaculation can sometimes be controlled by a woman-on-the-top position, because muscle tension sometimes plays a role in the problem. When you are on the bottom, you can be more relaxed and be responsible for less of the movements.

Therapy

Try therapy for premature ejaculation. The therapy for premature ejaculation is effective, easy, and quick - just a few weeks. No, it's not the extensive lay-on-the-couch-and-talk-about-your-childhood type of therapy. You are taught to know your body signals and how to control your ejaculations. Call your nearest sex therapy center. You may even be able to arrange for the therapy to done by phone.

MEMORY LOSS

Have you ever: Walked into a room and forgotten what you went there for? Searched in your mind for a name to match the face of the person before you? Forgotten a birthday or anniversary? Made a trip to the grocery store only to come home with "everything but what you set out to get?"

How you look at it

Memory lapses like these are laughed off when you're young. You don't give them a second thought. But, when you're over forty these amusing little lapses take on a sinister significance. Then everyone worries that they are harbingers of senility or Alzheimer's - "you're losing it."

Are you stuck with a poor memory?

Some people seem to have better memories than others. But according to a survey by the Roper Organization, 9 out of 10 people say they have poor memories. If you have a poor memory, are you stuck with it? No, the good news is you can improve your memory!

Organization - Everything in it's place

Often what's mistaken for poor memory is merely poor organization. If you're forever forgetting where you put things like keys or tools, maybe the problem isn't as much a memory problem as an organization problem. If your life is disorganized, rushed, frantic, you'll loose track of the little bits of information that tell you where you left things.

The solution here is to organize yourself - train yourself to be organized. Learn to put your keys and tools, whatever, where they belong.

Let's take the key problem, for instance. Decide on one place where your keys will be kept. To start with, you will have to pay attention and force yourself to put your keys in that spot each time after using them.

Soon your habit of dropping your keys any old place will be replaced by your new habit of putting them where they belong. And you'll find them easily the next time you need them. Like magic, it seems your memory has improved!

Attention - Lights, camera, action!

Think of yourself as an old-fashioned movie camera that requires lights. Your lights are regulated by your attention. When you're very interested and pay strict attention, your lights are bright and you get lots of details on your film. When you pay little attention the lights are dim and you only pick up a few scattered details.

Write it down

Writing down the things you want to remember helps you in several ways:

     (1) Sight reinforces the thought.
     (2) You give it more concentration and attention.
     (3) You can save the idea to concentrate on at a more
          convenient time.

Tips For students (and others)

Information retention is extremely important to students. The SQUIRT system works well for studying textbooks but can also be adapted to business reports, magazine articles, and other written materials.

First, you'll more easily learn and better retain anything that you enjoy and have a deep interest in. So try to approach the material without a sense of dread or reluctance.

And don't procrastinate! Last minute cramming makes for poor memory retention and poor tests. When you cram, you overload your memory circuits.

Using the Squirt System

Now, we're not talking about a little squirt here, but a long, drawn-out squirt like this - SQRRRT.

Imagine a water hose. You're not just sprinkling your friend; you're drenching him!

This is how the system works:

(S)   **Survey:** Take plenty of time. Look over the material; flip through the pages. Casually look over the table of contents, headings and subheadings, illustrations, and the summaries and questions at the end.

(Q)   **Question:** Skim lightly over the material and think about the key questions that emerge. Don't worry about the answers at this point.

(R)   **Read:** Now read over the material. Don't take any notes or do any highlighting. Just read.

(R)   **Recite:** As you go through the material this time, recite so you hear the important information. You don't have to recite loudly. Even whispering will work. Now is a good time to take notes or highlight important passages.

(R)   **Review:** Go over the material once again before putting it away.

(T)   **Time:** Give it a little time, a rest. Go back to the material a few days later and review it again.

Can memory be learned?

To a large extent memory is a learned activity. If you learn to be organized, to be interested and pay attention, and to approach memorization with a plan, you can certainly improve your retention level.

Overflowing filing cabinet

Your memory is like a filing cabinet full of information. Picture a filing cabinet overflowing with useful material. It's all just stuffed in there haphazardly. It could just as well be thrown into a big box.

Now you want to retrieve a particular bit of information. You'll have to dig through all that stuff to find it. Your chances of finding it in short order are pretty slim.

Neat filing cabinet

Now picture that cabinet with everything filed neatly and alphabetically. When you need a particular item, you can put your hands on it immediately because you already know the alphabet. The information is right where you expect it to be - filed under the proper letter cue.

Is your memory a big box or a filing cabinet?

Your memory works something like that. When you are exposed to new information, if you just throw it into a big box, you'll have trouble finding it again.

If you file the new information, cue it to something you already know, it'll be easier to find when you need it. And if you cross-reference it (cue it to more than one thing you already know), it will be even easier to retrieve.

A physical problem?

Your brain, of course, is a part of your physical body. So a poor or failing memory could be a physical problem.

The drawers are stuck

Like the rest of your body, your brain depends upon good blood circulation. Blood carries the "food" your brain feeds on. If your blood flow is impeded, your mind cannot work to its capacity and your mental processes unable to work as they should - you may have everything filed neatly but some of the drawers are stuck.

This is part of the problem when suffering from fear or extreme stress. You have difficulty thinking clearly because these emotions tend to constrict your blood vessels and impede your blood flow.

Keep those drawers working properly

Improving blood flow will help to keep those drawers working properly or get them to work better.

How do you that? First, a cardiac diet will help. Why? Because a cardiac diet discourages cholesterol build-up. Cholesterol build-up creates a sluggish blood flow.

Aerobic exercise strengthen your heart so it will pump better as well as lowering your cholesterol.

Niacin, a vitamin you can buy at any pharmacy, improves your blood flow and is used for treating poor circulation.

Ginkgo, an herb of Chinese origin, has been shown to dilate arteries, veins, and capillaries. Extracts of ginkgo are regularly prescribed in Asia and Europe to improve mental functions.

THE DREADED ALZHEIMER'S DISEASE

Alzheimer's disease has touched nearly everyone through family or friends. The hallmarks of Alzheimer's - loss of memory, loss of personality, and irreversible dementia - have made this a much dreaded disease.

The presence of aluminum

Research has revealed that aluminum is present in affected portions of Alzheimer-affected brains. And there is evidence that aluminum is poison to the nervous system. Does it seem strange to think of aluminum in your brain? In your body, aluminum is not a metal - just as iron in your body is not a metal. It is a mineral. Some researchers have advised avoiding aluminum whenever possible to reduce your chances of developing Alzheimer's disease.

Avoiding aluminum is impossible

Totally avoiding aluminum is impossible because aluminum is everywhere in our environment. Like iron, aluminum is ingested with the food we eat. Aluminum from the soil is absorbed into growing plants. Then we either consume those plants directly or through the meats of animals which have eaten the plants.

So what can you do?

So what can you do to decrease your chances of developing Alzheimer's disease? Although you can't avoid it completely, you can reduce the amount of aluminum your body is subjected to. Two sources that can be controlled are antacid medications and cosmetics.

Antacids

Some very popular and effective antacid medications contain aluminum compounds. But there are some very effective medications that do not contain aluminum. When choosing an antacid, check the labels.

Deodorants

Many deodorants and cosmetics contain aluminum. You may have to look a bit to find a deodorant or antiperspirant that does not. But, again, check the labels. There are some out there that are aluminum-free. Avoid all cosmetics that contain aluminum compounds.

BACK PAIN

At one time or another, you are likely to suffer from back pain. Nearly everyone does.

Causes

Poor posture, sitting in awkward positions, a sedentary lifestyle, poor back and abdominal muscle tone, and muscle strain can all cause back pain. Because nearly all movement radiates to or from your back, a painful back can be extremely debilitating.

Relieving your problem

If you are suffering from back pain, your medical doctor may not be the best person to consult. Treating your symptoms with pain relievers may bring relief, but doesn't address the cause.

Often a chiropractor is more effective in relieving your pain. A chiropractor will treat your problem with spinal adjustments. Or you may find a qualified massage practitioner will do wonders for you.

Yoga will strengthen and relax muscles and improve alignment and posture. But be careful. Some of the positions may be to strenuous for an ailing back. Deteriorating disks may benefit from vitamins C and E.

Some hints for avoiding or minimizing back pain

Practice good posture. Walk and stand with your back in alignment. Don't remain stationary when standing for a length of time. Switch your weight from leg to leg or prop one foot up on something like a chair rung.

Don't slouch in your chair or driver's seat. Sit on your buttocks with your back aligned. Use chairs with a firm seat and lower back support. Avoid crossing your legs when seated.

Learn and use proper methods of lifting and handling objects without strain.

Use daily, gentle exercises to tone back and abdominal muscles. Walking, swimming, rowing, and cycling are all good exercise for your back.

Don't engage in rough or jarring sports like football or tennis. Don't wear high heels exclusively.

Sleep on your back or side on a firm mattress with a pillow under your head. Vitamin D, calcium, and vitamin C are important in the development and health of bones and nerve functions.

VARICOSE VEINS

Avoid smoking, obesity, and standing for long periods. Take vitamins C and E and bioflavinoids. Horse chestnuts are used in a number of circulatory problems - varicose veins, blood clots, and hemorrhoids.

DEPRESSION

Depression can disrupt the sufferer's life. It can cause lack of sleep, fatigue, inability to concentrate, changes in appetite, irritability, and more. Depression is a serious illness and should be treated as such.

Could be caused by your medications

If you suffer from the blues for no apparent reason, it could be caused by medications that you may be taking. And symptoms may not appear right away. So don't rule out your medications simply because you've been on them for six months or a year. Some of the drugs that have been known to cause depression in some people are:

Oral contraceptives

The Pill often brings on feelings of depression. The depression is related to the dosage of hormones in the medication. Your doctor may be able to prescribe a different dosage or vitamin B6 therapy to counteract the depressive symptoms.

Antihistamines

These are prescribed for allergies - sneezing, runny nose, itchy skin, hives. Long term use can lead to depression. See your doctor about alternative medications.

Cortisone and other steroids

Often prescribed for asthma, arthritis, colitis, allergies, psoriasis, these drugs may be causing your depression. But DO NOT DISCONTINUE your medication without talking to your doctor. Discontinuing suddenly can cause very serious condition. Your doctor can advise you of other possible medications for your condition.

High blood pressure medications

Reserpine, methyldopa, clonodine, and beta-blockers all can cause depression symptoms in some patients. See your doctor if you are on these medications and are suffering from depression. DO NOT DISCONTUINUE your medication without a doctor's advise. Your doctor may be able switch you to other antihypertensives.

Heart medications

Some drugs prescribed for erratic heartbeat and congestive heart failure may cause depression in some people. Digitalis, often prescribed for arrythmic heartbeat, is known to affect some people. DO NOT DISCONTINUE your medication without consulting your doctor. Your doctor may decide to substitute another medication.

Glaucoma medication

Timolol may cause symptoms of depression. Consult your doctor if you're using these eye-drops and are depressed.

It may *not* be your medication

These drugs cause symptoms of depression in only a small percentage of the people using them. Don't automatically assume that the drugs you are taking are causing your depression. But if you are on one of these medications and are suffering from the blues, see your doctor and ask if the drug could be the culprit.

Fatigue

The concentrate made from the whole leaf of the aloe vera combats fatigue. In addition to dramatically increasing energy, drinking aloe vera will help you to sleep better and combat the symptoms of irritable bowel syndrome and other colon disease.

MENSTRUAL PROBLEMS

For PMS: Vitamin B complex, vitamin B6, folic acid, vitamin E, calcium, and magnesium. For water retention: Juniper berry tea works as a diuretic to relieve these symptoms. Caution: Do not use with damaged kidneys or if pregnant.

For cramps or abdominal discomfort: Massage bottoms of feet from instep back to heel. Drink chamomile tea steeped in a closed vessel for at least 10 minutes. Chew 2 or 3 leaves of feverfew daily.

Menopausal problems

Hot flashes, backache, and loss of bone mass: Vitamins E, C, B5, calcium, vitamin D, ginseng. Limit coffee and alcohol.

ASTHMA

Avoid getting close to trees, flowering shrubs, and plants during the pollen season. Avoid mowing the lawn. Avoid smoking and smoke filled rooms. Cover nose and mouth in very cold weather.

Practice deep breathing exercises. When exercising or playing sports opt for those that allow periods of rest rather than aerobic exercise which demands continued effort.

Vitamin A (in beta-carotene form), C, B6, B12, E, pantothenic acid, calcium, manganese, and magnesium. Peppermint tea will help to relieve the symptoms of asthma.

Arthritis

Daily exercise especially swimming exercises. Application of heat, soaking in warm bath. Application of oil of chamomile. Concentrate of whole leaf of aloe. Feverfew leaves - chew 2 to 3 leaves daily. Vitamins C and E and niacinamide. Zinc, copper, Vitamin B6, calcium pantothenate. Alfalfa tablets and fish oil.

Vitamins for youthful skin

The vitamins that are important to maintaining youthful skin include beta carotene, B complex, A, and C. These vitamins are found in abundance in fruits and vegetables. In the following charts an x indicates a good source for the vitamin it appears under.

Fruits	A	C	Bcmplx	Beta caro
Apricots	x			
Blueberries	x	x		
Cantaloupe	x	x		
Cherries	very high	x		
Grapefruit	x	high		
Guavas		very high		
Kiwi		high		
Kumquats		high	x	
Lemons		high		
Limes		x		
Mangos	very high	x		
Nectarines	high			
Oranges	x	very high		
Papaya	very high			
Peaches	high			
Pears	x	x		
Plums	x			
Strawberries		very high		
Tangelo		x		
Tangerines	x	x		
Watermelon	very high	x		

Vegetables

	A	C	B cmplx	Beta caro
Argula		x		
Asparagus	x	x		
Avocado	x	x		
Beans	x			
Beet tops	high			
Broccoli	x	high		
Brus Sprouts		high		
Cabbage		high		high
Carrots	high			very high
Cauliflower		high		
Collard grns	high	high		
Corn	x			

	A	C	Bcmplx	Beta caro
Endive	x			
Fennel	very high			
Kale	very high	x		
Kohlrabi		x		
Lettuce	x			
Mustard grns	high	high		
Okra	x	x		x
Peas	x			
Potatoes		x		
Pumpkin	very high			
Rutabaga	high	x		
Spinach	very high	high		
Sprouts	high			
Squash	x	x		
Swt potatoes	very high			
Swiss chard	very high			
Tomatoes	high	high		
Water cress	very high			

WEIGHT LOSS

Weight loss is no mystery. It is mathematical. When the body burns up more calories than it takes in, it uses the calories stored in the tissue.

Lose a pound

To lose one pound a week, you need to cut 500 calories a day or increase activity by 500 calories. Moderate exercise helps take off weight by speeding up your metabolic rate so calories are burned more quickly and efficiently.

Go slowly

Rapid weight loss is not advised. A rapid weight loss achieved from a very low-calorie and very low-carbohydrate diet comes from lean tissue and water because the body will burn proteins instead of breaking down fat.

A low-fat, high-carbohydrate diet, on the other hand, raises the ratio of lean body weight to fat. Exercise improves the ratio even further. It also helps burn calories.

Ratio of fat to lean and metabolization

With a higher ratio of fat to lean body weight, you will metabolize your food differently. If you are a flabby 220 pound executive, you don't need as many calories as a muscular 220 pound athlete.

Easy and convenient weight loss

What if you want to loose weight but don't have the time or inclination to count calories and fuss with special foods? A casual weight loss program can work - you simply need to burn more calories than you consume. To loose a couple of pounds per week, you need only increase your exercise moderately and cut a couple hundred calories from your diet.

Casual exercise

Increase your exercise easily by parking a little distance from your destination and walking. Take the stairs instead of the elevator. Take a quick walk around the block in the evening.

Casual Diet

Cutting a couple of hundred calories is as simple as toting up the average number of calories you consume for dinner and reducing your portions accordingly. You don't need to give up any foods you like and you don't have to count calories every day. For example, if your average dinner is about 800 calories, eat the same things - but eat three quarters of your usual amount. Your caloric intake will be reduced by a couple of hundred calories.

Casual magic

With this casual increase in exercise and casual cutting of dinner portions, you'll loose a couple of pounds a week with no formal exercise program, no calorie counting, no fussing with special foods, no eliminating of favorite foods!

Chromium picolinate

Chromium is an essential element of nutrition. It facilitates fat metabolism - helps you burn calories and build muscle.

WANT TO GET YOUR BOOK PUBLISHED

You thought you were over the big hurdle once you got the darn thing written. But now you're finding that no one seems interested in publishing it. What can you do?

Stay out of the closet

Well, first don't get discouraged - don't toss the thing onto the top shelf in your closet yet. Not getting published doesn't mean it's not a good book. Lots of good writing never sees the printed page.

"Only the experienced need apply."

Publishing's superhouses - the big guys in the publishing field - turn down most new authors. In fact, it may be difficult to even get a reading.

The major publishers see established writers as a "sure thing" and new authors as high risks. Many will publish a manuscript from a published writer in preference to a better one from an unknown.

It's rather like coming out of school ready to go to work only to find employers don't want to hire you until you get experience. It's frustrating. You keep asking yourself, "If no one will hire me, where do I get the experience?"

So where do you get the experience?

Okay, so it would be nice to jump right in with the big publishers. Immediate fame and fortune!

You've heard the stories - first book, instant smash hit, overnight success. Yes, it does happen. But very seldom. And overnight success in any field can be an illusion:

> Actually, I'm an overnight success. But it
> took twenty years.—Monty Hall

Start with smaller publishers

If the super houses turn you down, try the smaller ones. Smaller publishers with less overhead are happy with smaller returns. They're happy with a reasonable profit and don't expect to publish a list of national best sellers so are more willing to take a risk with a new author.

Four kinds of smaller houses

There are four kinds of smaller publishing houses that you should consider:

University presses - yes, they do publish books by non-scholars, but they must be deemed worthwhile and make a contribution to the world's knowledge.

Literary small presses - publish literary fiction and distinguished non-fiction.

Niche publishers - publish books restricted to a specialized field like photography, religion, gay issues, etc.

Mini majors - are similar to the major publishers in what they publish but aren't as large so they keep their overhead down.

Not a snap

These houses are not a snap. In fact, some may have standards tougher than the big houses. But they are more interested in quality and talent than experience. New authors, if they're good, have a chance.

Start with non-fiction

You can enhance your chances of getting published if you start with non-fiction, choosing a topic which is of current interest. These books require little advertising to generate decent sales reducing the risk the publisher is taking. Non-fiction readers often choose their books by subject and aren't as fussy about who the author is. Of course, an especially qualified person - historian, doctor, soldier, professor, businessperson - will be considered first.

The Most Valuable Book Ever Published

Start with category fiction

Category fiction is fiction aimed at the fans of particular genres. This includes westerns, romances, science fiction, fantasy, horror, etc.

Genre readers are likely to buy books based on the cover and the first few pages rather than national advertising. So like non-fiction, category fiction reduces the cash outlay risk for the publisher. Although big sellers are rare, the risk is minimal.

Enter Contests

Enter contests open to unpublished writers. Some of these contests are taken very seriously by publishers and a win could win you a contract.
Watch the writer's magazines and literary publications for contest announcements.

Join Mark Twain, Edgar Allen Poe, and Walt Whitman

Publishers are not infallible. They don't always recognize a winner. If they just don't recognize your talents, publish yourself. Some of our most respected authors - like Mark, Edgar, and Walt - have published their own books.

Self-publish

When you self-publish, you retain ownership of your book. Of course, at the same time, you take on the responsibility for the manufacture, promotion, and distribution, as well.

Some small publishers and book printers will manufacture your book for a fee. Many offer advise, editing, and proof reading services. Some even offer nominal promotion and distribution services.

Book printers can be found through the advertising directors of writer's magazines and literary publications. Or try the printers in your local area.

YOU'D LIKE TO SAVE SOME MONEY

You really would like to save some money. But you simply can't because it takes all you earn to live. If only you earned a little bit more, you could save regularly.

You aren't alone

Would you believe that people whose incomes are thousands more than yours are saying the same thing? Do you wonder why they can't save with incomes of that size?

Earnings versus attitude

Their problem is the same as yours - and it has little to do with earnings but a lot to do with attitude. Many people tend to live up to (or beyond) the extent of their incomes. If you have a few dollars in your pocket and a paycheck due on Friday, it's very difficult to resist buying something you want or feel you need. And when payday arrives, there is little or nothing left of the last paycheck. So how the heck do put anything into a savings account?

What would you do with a reduced income?
Ask yourself what you would do if your income was cut by twenty or thirty dollars a week. You know you'd survive it - in fact, many people live on a lot less. Would you get along without that you now spend that cash on?

Why not find out?

Perhaps the easiest way to save money is to cut your paycheck! Why not give it a try? Put money into savings as soon as you get your check - or better yet sign up for a payroll savings plan. And make up your mind that the savings will not be touched unless you're faced with an emergency. It's like cutting your paycheck. You will be forcing yourself to live on a little less income.

Look at it as a challenge

Making it a challenge or a game will help you get through the first few weeks. After that, you will find it easy - you will have adjusted to living on a little less and will probably not even think about it.

It gets easier

Even a small amount saved regularly will grow quite fast. You'll be amazed! And as the amount grows, it'll seem more and more important to keep it growing so it'll be easier to save.

Pledging your raises

You may even want to increase your regular contribution to your savings. An easy and painless method is pledging your raises. Decide in advance what percentage of each raise will go into savings. If you change your contribution immediately upon receiving your raise, you will never miss it!

NOTES

OTHER HEALTH AND MONEY BOOKS

The following books are offered to our preferred customers at a special price.

BOOK	PRICE	
1. Penny Stock Newsletter (12 issues)	$55.00	*POSTPAID*
2. Lower Cholesterol & Blood Pressure	$26.95	*POSTPAID*
3. Book of Home Remedies	$26.95	*POSTPAID*
4. Proven Health Tips Encyclopedia	$19.97	*POSTPAID*
5. Foods That Heal	$19.95	*POSTPAID*
6. Natural Healing Secrets	$26.95	*POSTPAID*
7. Most Valuable Book Ever Published	$16.95	*POSTPAID*
8. Eliminate Prostate Problems	$16.95	*POSTPAID*
9. Drugs-Side Effects	$16.95	*POSTPAID*
10. Govt. . Benefits For 50 or Over	$26.95	*POSTPAID*
11. Book of Credit Secrets	$26.95	*POSTPAID*
12. How To Win At Slot Machines	$30.00	*POSTPAID*
13. How To Trade Commodities	$149	*POSTPAID*
14. How To Trade Options	$149	*POSTPAID*
15. Money Power	$24.95	POSTPAID
16. Proven Wealth Creating Techniques And Formulas	$19.95	P0STPAID

Please send this entire page or write down the names of the books and mail it along with your payment

NAME OF BOOK_____PRICE_____
NAME OF BOOK_____PRICE_____
NAME OF BOOK_____PRICE_____
NAME OF BOOK_____PRICE_____

TOTAL ENCLOSED $_____

SHIP TO:
Name_____
Address_____
City_____ST_____Zip_____

MAIL TO: KEYSTONE PUBLISHING
POST OFFICE BOX 51488
ONTARIO, CA 91761-9827

For other fine books go to our website:

www.emarketupdate.com